PROMOTING GLOBAL TEACHER EDUCATION

Seven Reports

Edited by
Jean L. Easterly

N
W ⬥ E
S

Association of Teacher Educators

Reston, Virginia

The Association of Teacher Educators wishes to acknowledge
the Longview Foundation for partial funding of this publication.

About the Cover

The famous sculpture graphically interpreted on the cover is found in Brazil's new capitol, Brasilia. Symbolizing the interconnectedness of all the continents, the sculpture offers hope for future generations around the world.

Association of Teacher Educators
1900 Association Drive, Suite ATE
Reston, VA 22091

Developmental editing by Roy A. Edelfelt
Copy editing and production management by Margo Johnson
Edelfelt Johnson, Chapel Hill, North Carolina

Cover and text design by Susan Leeb
Susan Leeb Graphic Design, Chapel Hill, North Carolina

CONTENTS

IV

FOREWORD

A number of years ago I had the privilege of spending a few months in Central America working in a village that seemed to have been forgotten by humanity. I learned so much. Probably the most important lesson was that poverty devastates the mind and the soul even more than the body. My responsibility was to assist some teachers in more appropriately considering the relationship between an effective curriculum and human existence. I shall never forget that experience; it has enriched my life.

Most education institutions have at one time or another engaged in a global education effort through student programs, faculty exchanges, or research. Certainly the opportunity to learn about different cultures and societies profoundly affects the participants personally and professionally. Many students and faculty come back from such an adventure not only strengthened by what they have witnessed and experienced, but truly moved.

Our mass media permit us to shrink the world. An incident in Bosnia or Beirut is seen in Omaha and Detroit as it happens. Clearly we can now be part of an international community even without a jet plane.

As president of the Association of Teacher Educators, I have had the opportunity to visit our teacher education colleagues throughout Europe. I have learned that many of the problems that we face in the United States are similar to those that our colleagues in other lands confront. Our concern for the social and intellectual well-being of children is shared by educators throughout the world. We can learn from one another. Just as we are committed to the education of all our children, so are they committed to the education of all their children.

It is appropriate that ATE, which has a history of involvement in international and global education, should publish this monograph. Teacher education goes beyond boundaries. Preparing professionals for a changing world is a constant concern and commitment. We therefore encourage teacher educators to continue their research and service and teaching throughout the world. Our students and all those whom they serve will benefit through such experiences.

Leonard Kaplan
1993–94 President
Association of Teacher Educators

1
INTRODUCTION
Jean L. Easterly

In 1958 I came home from a summer in Europe, singing "Volare." To my surprise, people in the United States were singing it also. Today people all over the world are likely to be singing a catchy new song.

I spent summer 1992 in South America. This time I returned with the music of panpipes in my ears, their haunting melodies bringing back visions of soaring mountain peaks and isolated villages on the high plateaus (*altiplano*) of the Andes.

We visited Ecuador at the time of the harvest and eight days of celebration, when the men dance all night. The once-green, terraced hillsides had become brown, and dried cornstalks stood beside the mud walls of villages. I remember jolting along the country roads toward Peguche, a tiny adobe village high in the Andes. There we were welcomed into the home of Grandfather Maldonado, his son Antonio, Antonio's wife Fabiola, and their children. The floor of their home was earthen, and the rectangular, one-story building and inner courtyard served as their living quarters, their factory, and their showroom. Grandfather Maldonado proudly displayed his skills of hand-carding and spinning on the loom. As I watched him, I wondered, Why do I know so little about this indigenous people, the Otavalenos, who lived in the Andes long before the Incas came? Why is my knowledge of post-Columbian America so detailed and my knowledge of pre-Columbian America so scant?

I remember our visit to La Compania Church in Quito, with its grey, ornate exterior. The stone steps leading up to the entrance of the church were covered with beggars reaching out to all who entered. Inside we were overwhelmed by the contrast, for the interior is covered with gold—seven tons, it is claimed. Some say the church is the most beautiful one in the world, but I was ashamed to have brushed by those needy people on my way in to see the spectacle. How do I share my feelings of outrage and disgust so that others can understand?

At the Herrera Museum in Lima, Peru, 3,000 ceramic heads were on display. These pieces tell us much about what life was like before the Incas; they are a kind of substitute for modern-day photography. The Moches, who preceded the Incas, left no written word, but their ceramics have been used to unravel some of the secrets of their society. Archaeologists and historians are revising history daily, but our K–12 classrooms continue with business as usual. How do we bridge the knowledge gap? How do we teach future teachers and future generations of students that history continually unfolds its secrets?

My visit to the Amazon was overwhelming. Nowhere on earth is the challenge for the global community more apparent. There we find the largest river basin in the world. The rainforest in this great region lives more from the air, the rain, and its own decay than from the very poor soil in which it grows. A square mile of rainforest can contain up to 3,000 different species of vegetation—literally the pharmacy of the world. The message is clear: Teaching about the protection of our fragile environment must be high on the list of curricular goals for the K–12 classroom. In turn, future teachers must be prepared to meet the challenge of this interdisciplinary field.

While visiting the Amazon, we stayed in Manaus, in the heart of the rainforest, 600 miles from the nearest city in any direction. I remember lying one night on a canopied bed in an air-conditioned room, watching *Dances with Wolves* with Portuguese dubbed in. I appreciated the artificial environment that kept me comfortable and entertained, and I reflected on the technology that made it all possible. This technology connecting the global community is an ever-growing force with the power to unite, to inform, and to promote the good of all if it is used with care.

Brasilia, Brazil's new capital, was of special significance for me. It rises from a high plateau in the center of Brazil where 40 years ago there was only savannah.

Planned in the shape of a giant airplane, Brasilia is a monument to what can be accomplished when people dream. In the city is a famous sculpture, which has been graphically interpreted on the cover of this monograph. Symbolizing the interconnectedness of all the continents, it offers hope for future generations around the world: hope that we will come to respect and accept one another, hope that we will come to understand the effects of our decisions on our shrinking global village, hope that all people will come to share in the resources of the world.

My South American adventure stands in sharp contrast to my European "Grand Tour," during which I experienced the splendors of Western European art, music, and history. At that time (1958) my education had brought me an understanding of the world through European history and culture. My experience in Europe confirmed and connected with my first college year of liberal studies and the K–12 education that had preceded it.

In the intervening 35 years my world has expanded, and I am thankful. As a professor of teacher education, I want to share these new understandings in ways that open doors for teachers and for their students in turn. Global awareness represents profound social change. Ecologically we are bound together in ways that were not clearly understood in the past. Today communication networks allow us literally to see and hear the events of the world through the eyes and the ears of those experiencing them. Increasingly our lives are affected by the interdependence of complex economic, political, technological, and ecological systems, each operating at the global level.

DEFINITION OF GLOBAL EDUCATION

Global awareness should be a critical part of the formal education of every child if he or she is to become a citizen and a steward of our global community. However, the question for many is, What is global education? According to Kenneth Tye in his introduction to the Association for Supervision and Curriculum Development's 1991 Yearbook, *Global Education: From Thought to Action*, global education

> involves learning about those problems and issues that cut across national boundaries, and about the interconnectedness of systems—ecological, cultural, economic, political, and technological. Global education involves perspective taking—seeing things through the eyes and minds of others—and it means the realization that while individuals and groups may view life differently, they also have common needs and wants. (p. 5)

OVERVIEW OF THE SEVEN REPORTS

What do we mean when we say that we are globally aware? What does it mean to teach with a global perspective? What must we teacher educators do to prepare both ourselves and our students for this increasingly more complicated world order? The seven reports that follow address these questions from a number of perspectives:

• For teacher educators who want to discover the meaning of *global awareness*, there is Trudi Osnes-Taylor's account (Chapter 2) of her progress in a personal quest to become more globally aware. She also writes about expanding that quest to include the teacher education program at the University of St. Thomas in St. Paul, Minnesota, thus responding to the question of what teacher educators must do. Finally, she describes her work with the international teacher education community and the formulation of the Comparative Teacher Education Information Exchange, a network designed to assist teacher educators in making personal contacts across cultural boundaries.

• For teacher educators who want to prepare their students for an increasingly more complex global environment, there is James Mahan and Laura Stachowski's report (Chapter 3), which describes Indiana University–Bloomington's replicable Overseas Student Teaching Project. In the past 15 years, over 420 student teachers have been placed in the national schools of England, Scotland, Wales, the Republic of Ireland, New Zealand, and Australia. The authors identify the many important insights and the nontraditional and traditional sources of learning reported by preservice teachers as a result of living, teaching, and interacting in a foreign nation.

• For teacher educators who want to enlarge their own global perspectives, there is Elaine Jarchow's illustration (Chapter 4), which describes a faculty exchange program between New Mexico State University and Hamilton Teachers College in New Zealand. Set in the context of the Maori and English cultures, this program comes complete with morning and afternoon tea. Jarchow offers suggestions to make exchanges easier.

There is also Linda and Morgan Lambert's description (Chapter 5) of their two years in Cairo working on a curriculum reform project funded by the US Agency for International Development. Their project was at the very heart of curriculum change in Egypt. In describing it, they draw on the teaching strategy called synectics, which uses metaphors for contrast.

• For teacher educators who want insights into working with graduate students and experienced teachers, there is Patricia Betts Roach's case study (Chapter 6), which describes how she and her colleagues oriented a group of 11 Arkansas teachers for a trip to India and then journeyed to India with them. Eight of the teachers had not traveled very much; four of them were taking their first airplane ride. The evaluation of the trip suggests that preparation for traveling abroad is far more complex than people initially envision.

• For teacher educators who want to know what it means to teach with a global perspective, there is Diane Sudbury's contribution (Chapter 7), which describes her ethnically diverse seventh-grade world history class. With many students curious about their roots and heritages, she has expanded the traditionally European perspective on the Middle Ages to include viewpoints and attitudes from Africa, China, and Japan.

There is also Audrey Wright's report (Chapter 8), which presents the results of a survey of Swedish and American teachers on the implementation of global education in their classrooms. The study focused on identifying which group had implemented more of the goals of global education, which goals had received the most and the least attention, and how teachers had actually implemented the goals that they claimed to be pursuing.

·✦·

The authors share specific ways to enhance the global awareness of teacher educators in both higher education and public and private K–12 schools. Although only one of the reports directly involves students, all have implications for these future citizens of our global community. If we as teacher educators are to be perceptive and informed about our ever-changing and fascinating world, we must act as catalysts for increasing awareness and involvement.

REFERENCE

Tye, K. A. (1991). Introduction: The world at a crossroads. In K. A. Tye (Ed.), *Global education: From thought to action* (1991 Yearbook of the Association for Supervision and Curriculum Development, pp. 1–9). Alexandria, VA: Association for Supervision and Curriculum Development.

2
"GOING GLOBAL,"
ONE TEACHER EDUCATOR AT A TIME
Trudi A. Osnes-Taylor

Ready or not, we are *all* "going global." This chapter is directed at teacher educators who, like me, feel inadequate for the task. It is written to share the quest of one teacher educator struggling with the changes necessary to reflect a shrinking world; it is offered in the hope that my progress might be an encouragement to others who are in the beginning stages of going global.

I believe that *program* changes can come about only as *individuals* change. Internationalization of teacher preparation happens as each of us teacher educators widens our perspectives on where we fit into the bigger world.

It was 1988, I had turned 41, and midlife crisis was setting in. What unique contribution did I have to make? How would the world be different in some small way because I had lived here? After months of searching my soul and fighting the sense of helplessness that comes from recognizing how huge and interconnected the problems are, and how tiny and finite we as individual humans are, I discovered my niche. What I most wanted to do was to help make connections among people of different cultures. This choice was based on my belief that only through direct human-to-human contact did we stop thinking of people as representatives of groups and begin to respect them as unique individuals; that only as we respected each other across cultural and political boundaries did we have hope of working together to solve problems.

My influence might be tiny, but I had a 24-hour day in which to operate. The best part of getting older was knowing that even those who acted as if they had all the answers, did not. As a teacher educator, I felt that I was in a good position to effect systemic change.

However, what resources did I have to share? I felt inadequate to join the conversations of faculty arguing about international issues. Even with my students, I felt ill equipped. Within just the past few years, the society around me and especially the Twin Cities schools had changed greatly. At the University of St. Thomas (in St. Paul, Minnesota), I was being called on to prepare 20-year-old undergraduates, most from suburban, relatively homogeneous settings, for classrooms in which children might speak 15 different languages and come from hugely varied and rich backgrounds. Except for a brief trip to Jamaica as a student, I had not been out of the country as an adult. Moreover, nothing that I could recall from my master's or doctoral programs had prepared me for educating myself or my classes to reflect the changing reality of the world.

A simple truism became increasingly clear to me: We teach what we *are*. I was not comfortable as a global citizen. I had to become global myself before I could expect to infuse an international perspective into my work. Each St. Thomas student is on an individualized Personal and Professional Development Plan (PPDP). I knew that I needed my own two- to three-year PPDP concentrating on international resources. The result included personal, programmatic, and professional components.

GLOBALIZING MY PERSONAL LIFE

In globalizing my personal life, I focused on three areas: increasing my knowledge base on global issues, traveling, and widening my personal contacts.

Increasing My Knowledge Base on Global Issues

First, I made slight changes in my daily patterns to become more aware of global issues. In addition to deliberately increasing my reading and discussions on international topics and spending more of my time watching international news shows, I started to listen to the public radio talk station regularly on my drive to and from work. (Now I am beginning to know how little I know—a major step in the process.)

Traveling

Surprisingly, the toughest problem for me in globalizing my personal life has been admitting my own ethnocentricity and fear level, particularly about overseas travel. College professors are supposed to be sophisticated; instead, I was intimidated. What if I offended someone of another culture by my ignorance? Would I look just like every other much-maligned American tourist? Could I learn anything in the short periods I had available?

Five years and six international trips later, I feel much more comfortable with myself. I have made a start. The first trip was with a tour, leaving the driving and the luggage problems to a delightful guide. By the third trip, flying through Tokyo into Taipei for a conference, arriving alone at midnight, I was proudly saying to myself, "I can do it!" Having been severely bitten by the international travel bug, I now recommend to my friends that they do whatever it takes to go almost anywhere. Although after a short trip we can make no claims to understanding another culture, we can at least gain an appreciation for other ways of doing things.

Widening My Personal Contacts

Like most of my teacher educator friends, I have neither unlimited funds nor much discretionary time for extended travel. However, recognizing the cursory nature of my overseas encounters, I realized that I had to have more extended contact with persons from other cultures. Through newspaper advertisements I learned about Nacel Cultural Exchanges, a student exchange program with US headquarters in St. Paul. Subsequently my family hosted a charming, bright French teenager for a summer. This past school year we hosted a German youth, from whom we learned an enormous respect for German family life, education, and politics. Both of their families have since visited us, and we have visited them. Additionally we have made special efforts to get to know other exchange students and neighbors from other countries. As a result, I have become far more reflective about everyday things that I used to take for granted.

GLOBALIZING THE TEACHER EDUCATION PROGRAM

As teacher educators become more globally connected, our teaching changes and our programs change.

Identifying Resources

I was amazed when I began to look at the resources available for infusing an international perspective into the St. Thomas teacher education program:

- *Faculty and staff inside and outside our department who have international connections.* The Business and International Languages departments have been especially helpful.
- *New faculty.* As new faculty have been hired in the department over the past two years, a factor in selection has been the global perspective and the global connections of the candidates.
- *The International Education Center on campus.* It was amazing, but our department had never sought the center's help before. Better advertising of its continuing international short courses has helped our students take advantage of opportunities to study abroad. Additionally I have become connected with a university-wide committee charged with internationalizing the campus.
- *Local ethnic organizations with connections in their homelands.*
- *International students at the university and in area K–12 exchange programs.*
- *The Minnesota State Department of Education.* A few calls produced many usable materials.
- *The campus library.* A quick search revealed excellent books on how to go overseas for long and short stays (e.g., *Academic Year Abroad,* published by the Institute of International Education, which will whet the appetite for travel) and on what was happening elsewhere (e.g., ATE's "Teacher Education: Perspectives from Abroad," *Action in Teacher Education,* Fall 1991; Willard Kniep's *Next Steps in Global Education: A Handbook for Curriculum Development;* and the American Association of Colleges for Teacher Education's *State of the Profession: International Field/ Student Teaching Experiences in Teacher Preparation*).
- *Established international programs.* Because reinventing workable wheels takes time, we have chosen to take advantage of a variety of continuing international student opportunities. The staff of Howard Freeberg's well-established and much-respected Student Teaching Abroad (STA) program has graciously allowed us to participate in their program until we have the opportunity to begin our own overseas programs. STA has been profoundly successful for a number of our students.
- *International teacher organizations.* Long-established organizations like ATE and the International Council on Education for Teachers (ICET) have a variety of materials that have been helpful in setting our directions.

Changing the Curriculum

Starting with the areas that were most in our control and had the least-immediate implications for the budget, the department added a course entitled Teacher as Global Citizen (a variation of the Human Relations course) and a required reflective multicultural experience as a program component. Long-range plans include developing our own overseas programs to allow our faculty to participate on a rotating basis, connecting with a growing number of international teacher educator networks, and increasing our technological capability. Our recent connections with Internet have already made a difference in bridging the distance and the time gaps between us and our international colleagues. We have found the fax machine to be particularly helpful in communicating with colleagues in other time zones. Each term we make progress.

GOING GLOBAL IN THE TEACHER EDUCATION PROFESSION

Recognizing the limitations of my personal experiences in connecting with the international teacher education community, I sought help.

Mentoring

I have learned the power of having a mentor. Like many women in my age group, I struggled through my graduate work and years of teaching, balancing home, children's needs, and study, and did not take the time necessary to build my own support system. It was quicker to do everything myself. Now, however, I needed help.

Whom did I know whose program reflected a truly international perspective? Whose work did I admire? One of my heroes was Howard Freeberg, who had spent 20 years connecting student teachers with placements around the world. A person who was working with Dr. Freeberg was a friend of mine, Craig Kissock of the University of Minnesota, Morris. Dr. Kissock was willing to work with me.

Defining Comparative Teacher Education

From our first meetings and after considerable review of the literature, Dr. Kissock and I prepared two papers for the International Seminar in Teacher Education (ISTE) in Prague. The first paper was an essay describing what we believed to be appropriate dimensions for the emerging field that we called comparative teacher education. The second paper described a process by which to add massive amounts of information to the database on comparative teacher education.

Developing the Comparative Teacher Education Information Exchange

The process described in the second paper was to evolve into the Comparative Teacher Education Information Exchange (CTEIEX). We asked teacher educators from many countries to help us refine a data-collection procedure based on the question, "What do teacher educators need to know about each other and each other's programs to begin to work together?" Starting with a 10-page questionnaire that included demographic information from documents of the United Nations Educational, Scientific, and Cultural Organization (UNESCO) and program-description dimensions from the newly revised standards of the National Council for Accreditation of Teacher Education (NCATE), we sought advice from teacher educators about how to describe our programs usefully for others to understand. Through a series of 20 or so meetings with teacher educators from over 40 countries between 1988 and 1992, at meetings of AACTE, ATE, ICET, and ISTE in Paris, Prague, and Taiwan, we refined the process. The product was very deliberately both the resultant two-page survey form and the friendships that developed over the hours of arguing about what should or should not go into the survey form.

An invitation to participate: Teacher educators in postsecondary education are invited to complete the CTEIEX form and participate in the information exchange. (Teacher educators in K–12 settings who are interested in organizing a similar exchange are welcome to contact me.) The kinds of information requested are name, address (home, work, and E-mail), and telephone and fax numbers; position; characteristics of the participant's institution and teacher education programs; opportunities at the participant's institution for faculty from other countries (e.g., teaching exchanges, guest lectureships, and joint research); and types of interchange in which the participant would be interested (e.g., short-term visits, student teacher exchanges, and home exchanges). The form may be obtained by contacting Dr. Trudi A. Osnes-Taylor, University of St. Thomas CHC131, 2115 Summit Avenue, St. Paul, MN 55110, USA, telephone 612/962-5412, fax 612/962-5789.

When the forms are submitted each year, they are collected, photocopied, organized by country, bound, and sent back to each person involved that year. Because of a small grant, there has so far been no charge for duplicating and mailing. The only requirement is that each participant contact at least one other teacher educator listed sometime over the year. Participants should feel free to pass the forms on to other teacher educators who are also going global, particularly those in other countries.

CONCLUSION

Going global is a task that no one of us will ever complete. Nor will it ever be completed at the University of St. Thomas or at any teacher preparation institution. In reality the process is the product. By letting our students share our intentions and reflect with us in our efforts to make ourselves relevant, globally sensitive educators, we model what we hope they will bring in turn to their students.

SELECTED RESOURCES

American Association of Colleges for Teacher Education. (1983). *A global perspective for teacher education* [Pamphlet]. Washington, DC: Author.

Banks, J. A. (1991). *Multiethnic education: Theory and practice.* Boston: Allyn and Bacon.

Churukian, G. A., & Kissock, C. (Eds.). (1991, Fall). Teacher education: Perspectives from abroad [Special issue]. *Action in Teacher Education, 13*(3).

Howard, E. E. (Ed.) (1990). *Academic year abroad.* New York: Institute of International Education.

Kennedy Center for International Studies. (1985). *Internationalizing: Critical considerations for success* [Infogram]. Provo, Utah: Brigham Young University.

Kniep, W. M. (Ed.). (1987). *Next steps in global education: A handbook for curriculum development.* New York: American Forum.

Lorenzo, M. (1990). *Microcomputer-based telecommunications: Implications for preservice teacher education* [Paper presented at the International Seminar for Teacher Education]. Taipei, Taiwan: Ming Teh Foundation.

Minnesota State Board of Education. (1988). Multicultural and gender-fair curriculum. *Minnesota Rules* 3500.0550.

Minnesota's vision for teacher education: Stronger standards, new partnerships [Report of the Task Force on Teacher Education for Minnesota's Future]. (1986). St. Paul, MN: Board of Teaching.

National Council for the Social Studies. (1983). *Curriculum guidelines* [Pamphlet]. Washington, DC: Author.

Osnes, T. (Ed.) (1991). *Comparative teacher education information exchange.* St. Paul, MN: Barcus Trust.

Osnes, T., & Kissock, C. (1989). *The cooperative development of a standard research instrument for the cross-cultural comparison of teacher education programs* [Paper presented at the International Seminar for Teacher Education]. Prague, Czechoslovakia: European Information Centre of Charles University for Further Education of Teachers.

Sharpes, D. (1988). *International perspectives on teacher education.* London: Routledge.

Sisney, S. (1989). Teacher leadership in reforming education. In *Preparing schools for the '90's.* New York: Metropolitan Life.

West, B. B. (1985). *The state of the profession: International field/student teaching experiences in undergraduate teacher preparation* [Working document]. East Lansing, MI: Michigan State University, College of Education.

3
THE MANY VALUES OF INTERNATIONAL TEACHING AND STUDY EXPERIENCES FOR TEACHER EDUCATION MAJORS
James M. Mahan and Laura L. Stachowski

As teacher education institutions across the United States strive to infuse elements of global education into their curricula, international teaching and study experiences are emerging as a viable means of developing a broader world perspective in preservice teachers. Such experiences serve to immerse novice educators in cultures outside the United States through classroom teaching practice, home living, required interviews with diverse foreign citizens, and community involvement. When these international experiences are prefaced by in-depth preparation for the host culture and education system and marked by continuing analysis and reflection, participants are likely to achieve personal and professional outcomes that could not be matched had they chosen to remain at home and complete conventional student teaching assignments. Documentation of these outcomes conveys to teacher educators nationwide that international experiences result in important new learnings, increased global understanding, and insight into ways that this knowledge can be incorporated into US elementary and secondary classrooms. Such data should serve to justify the investment of human and financial resources in international programs and to motivate and encourage teacher educators to attempt similar programs at their respective institutions.

The Overseas Student Teaching Project at Indiana University–Bloomington has been the source of considerable data on the outcomes of international field experiences. Some of these data are the focus of this chapter. It will be evident to the reader that preservice educators who teach, live, study, communicate, and participate in international schools and communities achieve a unique blend of learnings pertaining to life in the world, global concerns, the act of teaching, and their own capacities, both professionally and personally.

INTERNATIONAL FIELD AND STUDY EXPERIENCES: GOALS, OBJECTIVES, AND OUTCOMES

The credibility of any educational endeavor lies partially in the goals and the objectives set forth by program planners and developers. Important, attainable goals and objectives serve as a selling point to program funders and potential participants. They also aid planners and developers in measuring the success of the endeavor. Programs offering international teaching and study experiences are no exception; in fact, the inclusion of strong goals and objectives is crucial in justifying the added expenses that such programs typically present.

The literature contains several statements of purpose outlined by teacher educators who offer international teaching and study opportunities. Notwithstanding minor variations, these intended outcomes seem to converge on expanded world horizons, increased world-mindedness, and better classroom teaching upon returning home (e.g., Baker, 1985; Cole & Mulder, 1983; Korsgaard, 1989; West, 1985; Wheeler, 1985). However, one may wonder to what extent these desired outcomes are actually achieved at the conclusion of an international field experience, and further, what *student teachers themselves* report that they have learned, achieved, and acquired, and how *they* believe that they have changed through the process of teaching, living, and studying in a foreign setting.

The vast majority of articles suggest that positive learnings, changes, and insights are the most common outcomes of international teaching experiences for preservice educators. Barnhart (1989), for example, found that participants in Iowa State University's Student Teaching Abroad Program reported the most growth occurring in life enhancement and affective areas, as opposed to cognitive areas. These results are not surprising, given the experiential nature of the international teaching experience. Kelleher and Williams (1986) found that participants in the Memorial

University of Newfoundland program believed their professional competence to have been further developed as a result of student teaching in England.

Through the Overseas Student Teaching Project at Indiana University–Bloomington, data have been collected annually on the outcomes of student teaching in international settings. For example, Mahan and Stachowski (1985) asked participants to identify and describe important teaching changes that they felt were the result of experiences in schools abroad. Dramatic growth and development were reported in the areas of selection and creation of curricular materials, professional interactions with colleagues, classroom management and discipline, student motivation, choice and use of instructional activities, self-evaluation efforts, content knowledge, evaluation of student learning, and lesson planning. Additionally Mahan and Stachowski found that overseas experiences led participants to believe that significantly more attention to global and international topics was needed in teacher education. These beliefs emerged after students had lived and taught in nations where many people (including school children) were able to carry on more in-depth and informed conversations about world affairs and concerns than their US counterparts.

Thus the literature provides a reasonable account of the value inherent in international field experiences, their goals and objectives, and the benefits accrued by US student teachers. A closer examination of *specific, student-reported* outcomes achieved by participants in Indiana University's project supports the role that such programs can play in the continuing preparation of preservice teachers and in the efforts to globalize teacher education curricula.

THE OVERSEAS STUDENT TEACHING PROJECT: A BRIEF DESCRIPTION

The Overseas Student Teaching Project has been operating for the past 15 years at Indiana University–Bloomington. Offered as an optional supplement to conventional student teaching, this increasingly popular project has placed over 420 student teachers in assignments in the national schools of England, Scotland, Wales, the Republic of Ireland, New Zealand, and Australia. Project participants undergo extensive preparation for their international experiences, including enrollment in a seminar and completion of several reading and writing assignments. Educational, cultural, social, and political topics relative to the host nations, as well as important global and international issues relevant to inhabitants of all countries, are the focus of these preparatory activities. Further, to receive state certification, project participants must student-teach in the state for a minimum of 10 weeks before going abroad.

Once in the overseas host school, project participants are expected to engage in all teacher-related functions of the school, to form friendships with community people and become involved in their activities, to interview people from diverse walks of life, and to submit reflective reports identifying local attitudes, cultural values, world issues of current concern in the host nation, and personal and professional insights. A minimum of 40 teaching days is required in the overseas school and community. Given various school holidays, approximately 10 weeks are necessary to fulfill the assignment. For a complete description of Indiana's program, the reader is referred to Mahan and Stachowski (1985).

Considerable data on the personal and professional outcomes achieved by project participants have been collected by means of in-depth surveys, reflective essay questions, visits by project staff to the overseas sites, and follow-up conferences on the participants' return home. In all cases, specificity in response is required; generalities such as "I learned a lot about myself" are discouraged, and students are asked to explain specifically *what* has been learned, changed, or achieved. Some selected outcomes are described in the following sections.

TYPES OF LEARNINGS REPORTED BY OVERSEAS STUDENT TEACHERS

Near the conclusion of their international field experiences, the student teachers are asked to reflect on, identify, and record new learnings that they judge to be very important personally or professionally. The reported types of learnings and their frequencies, compiled for 63 participants in recent semesters, appear in Table 3-1. The 63 participants reported 1,688 highly valued learnings, an average of 26.79 per individual.

Perhaps the most noteworthy trend in Table 3-1 is that only 29.2% of these learnings were classified by overseas student teachers into the Classroom Teaching Strategies and Curriculum Content/Selection/Usage categories, the common foci for teacher education courses. Vital as such skills and knowledge are to effective teaching, they need not rule out important learnings of a different nature that can be garnered during an international student teaching experience (or a culturally different domestic one). These more extensive and diverse factual and affective learnings in the categories listed in Table 3-1 are typically not addressed in conventional student teaching, nor are novice educators generally required to engage in activities that would make such learnings possible. Yet the overseas student teachers for whom these learnings became reality attach major importance to them. Discoveries about self and the relationship of self to others and to the world appear to be

TABLE 3-1
LEARNINGS REPORTED BY OVERSEAS STUDENT TEACHERS,
BY CATEGORY

$\overline{X}$ Learnings per Respondent	Category of Learning	% of Total Responses ($N = 1,688$)
4.17	Classroom teaching strategies	15.6
3.79	Self-discoveries	14.2
3.65	Understanding/relating to people	13.6
3.65	Curriculum content/selection/usage	13.6
3.40	Facts not related to teaching	12.7
3.38	World human life/global issues	12.6
3.06	Aesthetics	11.4
1.68	Miscellaneous	6.3

highly valued, suggesting that significant learning does occur outside the classroom when it is structured into a student teaching program.

Some samples of the types of learnings reported by project participants are presented in Table 3-2. The samples serve to illustrate the breadth of the participants' exposure, their inclusion of more community and world perspectives and influences, and their attention to facts, issues, and relationships that many if not most conventional student teachers have seldom revealed via field experience research articles.

A strong link has been formed between overseas student teaching and global learnings, in response to the recognized need for more globally literate educators in the US workforce. By the conclusion of the international experience, each participant has been required to prepare and submit four in-depth essays on important global or international topics or issues, including their application to classroom teaching. The student teachers have generated a large number and a wide variety of essay topics. A brief sampling follows:

Antarctica and the Antarctic treaty

Arms reduction

Chemical weapons

Decline of Communism in Eastern Europe and the USSR

Deforestation and destruction of rainforests

Depletion of the ozone layer

Endangerment of plants and animals

Human freedom and human rights

International migration of people

Need to increase use of public transportation

Nuclear weapons, nuclear testing, and nuclear power

Pollution and environmental destruction

Race and ethnic relations

Terrorism

World hunger

TABLE 3-2
SAMPLE LEARNINGS REPORTED BY OVERSEAS
STUDENT TEACHERS

Teaching strategies	"Many of the children in my class are recent immigrants to Australia, and English is not their first language. I quickly learned the importance of using visual aids and teacher modeling with those pupils. In the United States, available teaching jobs tend to be in areas heavily populated by minorities. I've acquired some valuable skills for teaching children who do not speak standard English. I have also learned how beneficial it is to actively involve my pupils in the assessment of their own academic achievement through the continuous construction of personal portfolios containing what they feel best represents their learning, thinking, and creating."
Curriculum	"British teachers are concerned about getting creative responses from their pupils instead of concentrating on memorization, identification, and topic comprehension. They probe their students through synthesis and evaluation. Worksheets and workbooks are virtually nonexistent; consequently, learning activities are much more stimulating, hands-on, and effective."
Factual learnings	"The people I've met in Scotland tend to be more concerned with the quality of life rather than the quantity of 'things' acquired in life. Cars, clothes, big homes, etc., are not as important to people here as they are at home. . . . Much more emphasis is placed on the conservation of this precious planet. People perceive the earth as our home, not our personal landfill or our personal warehouse."
Human relationships	"I learned that in many cultures, the most respected people are not necessarily the wealthiest or most educated. Status in the community is defined in very different terms than it is in the United States. For example, one of the most respected people in Sneem [Ireland] is a gentleman who didn't go to school past the age of 16. He is admired for his generosity and his willingness to help anyone in the community, if he is able, including children."
Self-learnings	"Living and teaching in Ashburton [New Zealand] has been the single most important step I could have taken in furthering my professional capabilities and knowledge, as well as challenging my personal values, beliefs, and current perspectives. For example, I became more aware of the world as a global unit instead of a world which caters primarily to the United States."
Aesthetics	"I saw the beauty in the Roman ruins in England and felt very moved by the history, lives, and goals buried beneath the stones, and wondered which of my favorite US buildings might in some future century radiate their beauty only from a state of ruin or neglect or catastrophe. It could happen to us."
Global issues	"I realized how important it is for people all over the world to work for the same goals. Only through worldwide efforts can environmental disasters be averted and can world democracy and freedom be obtained and ultimately maintained. For example, how many nuclear 'things' are reasonable, and should any part of this world be sacrificed as the storage bin for nuclear waste?"

TABLE 3-3
SOURCES OF LEARNING IDENTIFIED BY OVERSEAS
STUDENT TEACHERS

Source of Learning	% of Total Sources Cited ($N = 2,459$)
School professionals: supervising/other teachers, principals, central office staff	38.6
Community people: nonschool community people, host-nation family, nonteacher school staff, parents of students, host-nation celebrities/leaders	34.4
School children in own and other classrooms	10.9
Listening, reading, reflecting: media, host-nation authors, self, preparatory workshop consultants	8.7
Physical things: land/weather/geography, museums/works of art	7.4

SOURCES OF LEARNINGS REPORTED BY OVERSEAS STUDENT TEACHERS

In considering the important new learnings gained by participants in international teaching, study, and living experiences, the teacher educator should also give attention to the sources of their learnings. A trend likely to emerge is that classroom teachers and university supervisors are not always the major influencers of student teachers' learning; nontraditional, noneducator sources also figure prominently and support the stance that the student teaching experience *should* extend beyond the walls of the classroom and the grounds of the elementary or secondary school. Table 3-3 indicates the sources of the important learnings that are listed by category in Table 3-1.

The fact that nonschool entities account for 50.5% of the student teachers' learnings is significant. The world beyond the doors of the school is used as a resource rich in new facts, discoveries, and understandings. Host families; employees at local shops; the farmer down the road; people at the nearby community center, church, or pub—all become important sources of learning for the student teachers, who are required to make new friends, socialize, help with the daily tasks of life, and learn more about the culture in which they have chosen to teach and live for several weeks. Further, cathedrals, castles, museums, local and national television and newspapers, ceremonies and celebrations, and other nonhuman sources are contributors to the knowledge acquired by overseas student teachers. Thus the student teaching experience can and should capitalize on all available sources of learning, both the traditional and time-proven education sources and the people, the objects, and the events that generally receive little or no recognition in the research and the literature.

TEACHING SKILLS, PROCEDURES, AND KNOWLEDGE IDENTIFIED AS NEEDING FURTHER DEVELOPMENT

A final area of student teacher–reported outcomes to consider involves the professional qualities that emerge at the conclusion of the overseas student teaching experience as being in need of further development. Data on these perceived deficits were obtained by means of an essay in which participants were asked to analyze critically their own teaching abilities and to identify specifically the teaching skills, procedures, and knowledge that they most wanted to make a stronger part of their professional repertoires. The essays of 120 student teachers were examined, with the skills, procedures, and knowledge grouped according to similar content, as shown in Table 3-4. The 120 student teachers identified 706 skills, procedures, and areas of knowledge to develop further, an average of 5.9 per individual.

Interestingly, even with extended, supervised practice in at least two different US and overseas classrooms, project participants continue to harbor concerns about such skills as classroom discipline, lesson planning, and student evaluation. Through increased awareness of their professional abilities, these student teachers exhibit a willingness thoughtfully and critically to assess their own teaching and to target the specific areas that require further development and growth. Also, they recognize the value of their overseas assignments—unique opportunities to depart from the way in which things are done at home and to try their hand at something new. Student teaching overseas undoubtedly raises questions in the participants' minds about their own effectiveness, their capabilities to enter the teaching profession with the drive, the dedication, and the repertoire of professional skills and professional adaptation mechanisms needed to become a master teacher of youth anywhere in the world.

CONCLUSION

The outcomes of international teaching, living, and study experiences for preservice educators tend to be encouraging. Such experiences have the potential to arm beginning US educators with new teaching ideas, skills, strategies, knowledge, and world perceptions that conventional student teaching programs are less likely to provide. By immersing themselves for several weeks in schools, homes, and communities where things are done differently, student teachers inevitably experience personal and professional changes usually leading to insights that might never have surfaced, learnings that no book can supply, and a professional self-portrait that

TABLE 3-4
TEACHING SKILLS, PROCEDURES, AND KNOWLEDGE IN NEED
OF FURTHER DEVELOPMENT

Skill/Procedure to Change	% of Respondents ($N = 120$)
Effective classroom discipline	90
Meeting individual learning needs	8
Lesson planning	43
Devising and using appropriate evaluation methods and standards	40
Specific teaching ideas to incorporate into classrooms back home	40
Integrated, thematic instruction	37
Communication and interaction with professional colleagues	37
Increased general and content knowledge	36
Organization and time management	23
Increased motivation (of both student teachers and children)	22
Flexibility in teaching	20
Setting expectations for students' achievement	17
Displaying students' work	17
Increased self-confidence in abilities as an educator	13
Use of cooperative learning	13
Parental involvement in students' education	12
Improvement as a leader or facilitator of learning	12
Continued learning/growth as a professional	10

in-state experiences alone cannot reveal. Student teachers also gain a broader perspective on the world, on other peoples who inhabit this planet, and on what it means to be teachers of elementary and secondary students who will be the custodians of our earth tomorrow.

REFERENCES

Baker, F. J. (1985). Alternative student teaching: Boon or boondoggle? *The Clearing House, 58*, 285–286.

Barnhart, R. S. (1989). The assessment of growth resulting from a student teaching experience in an international setting. *International Education, 18*(2), 5–13.

Cole, D. J., & Mulder, R. L. (1983, July). *Developing an international education program in pre-service teacher training.* Paper presented at the World Assembly of the International Council on Education for Teaching, Washington, DC. (ERIC Document Reproduction Service No. ED 232 988)

Kelleher, R. R., & Williams, L. E. (1986). Cross-cultural student teaching: An assessment of a Newfoundland program. *Education Canada, 26*(2), 30–35.

Korsgaard, R. (1989). *Overseas practice teaching.* River Falls, WI: Foundation for International Education.

Mahan, J. M., & Stachowski, L. L. (1985). Overseas student teaching: A model, important outcomes, recommendations. *International Education, 15*(1), 9–28.

West, B. B. (Ed.) (1985). *The state of the profession: International field/student teaching experiences in undergraduate teacher preparation—Images for the near future.* Paper commissioned by the American Association of Colleges for Teacher Education for the Guidelines for International Teacher Education Project. (ERIC Document Reproduction Service No. ED 265 113)

Wheeler, A. H. (1985, Nov.). *Beyond the crossroads: Charting the future.* Initial address to the faculty of the College of Education and Behavioral Science, Southeast Missouri State University. (ERIC Document Reproduction Service No. ED 265 154)

4

NEW MEXICO/NEW ZEALAND FACULTY EXCHANGES TO ENHANCE INTERNATIONAL AWARENESS

Elaine Jarchow

International faculty exchanges have a transforming effect on the individual scholars who participate and can also transform the institution to which they return. (Mossberg, 1990, p. 44)

Why foster faculty exchanges? In *Exchange 2000* the Liaison Group for International Educational Exchange (1989) notes,

The traditional mission of United States exchange programs has been to meet five major policy objectives:
1. To foster international peace and mutual understanding.
2. To build cooperative international networks of individuals and institutions.
3. To strengthen U.S. understanding of major world regions and specific nations, particularly at senior academic levels.
4. To apply U.S. educational resources to the development of the human resources of developing nations.

5. To encourage current and future leaders' understanding of U.S. values and culture through direct exposure to U.S. institutions. (p. 4)

The group suggests that exchange goals for the 1990s and beyond should be as follows:

1. Increase public awareness about our growing need for international competence and develop a national action plan.
2. Build U.S. international skills through expanded international exchanges.
3. Use exchanges to establish the common base of knowledge needed to address global problems.
4. Support human resources development for less developed nations.
5. Promote international cultural understanding through strengthened exchanges in the arts. (pp. 5–9)

Barbara Burn (1988), director of international programs at the University of Massachusetts at Amherst, concludes that faculty exchanges have the potential significantly to internationalize the curriculum. She cites a survey of more than 3,000 former Fulbright scholars that yielded the following findings:

> Some 80% of grantees formed permanent friendships abroad, while 70% have since their grant visited friends abroad, changed their "world view." Sustained commitment to international involvement is further reflected in the fact that 54% are members of local groups involved in foreign affairs education, over 40% assist Fulbrighters in their area, nearly 20% have served as foreign student adviser at their institutions, and 12.5% as Fulbright adviser. Former Fulbrighters are evidently concerned to keep in their own lives and share with others the kind of cross-cultural experience which is so central to the Fulbright experience. (p. 33)

Echoing the potential of faculty exchanges, Mossberg (1990) states, "International experience should be a requisite for our faculty members" (p. 44). She encourages institutions to provide vehicles to capitalize on and use the contributions of the returning faculty members.

In their paper entitled "Extending Boundaries: Narratives on Exchange," Cole and Knowles (1992) comment, "Exchange programs are promoted as ways of providing opportunities for developing broadened perspectives . . . They help develop sympathetic perspectives of the cultures and daily experiences of citizens of other countries" (p. 58).

A SEMESTER IN NEW ZEALAND

My fall 1990 semester faculty exchange with Clive McGee, Hamilton Teachers College, Hamilton, New Zealand, was a truly enriching experience for me, my family, and New Mexico State University (NMSU). Fortunately NMSU and Hamilton Teachers College have a dynamic relationship consisting of faculty and student exchanges as well as joint research projects. The faculty exchange is relatively easy to accomplish once appropriate administrative approvals are on file. Each faculty member earns his or her own salary and trades a house, a car, and a job. Each agrees to pay the other's utilities. Sometimes, airfare assistance can be obtained from the home department.

Teaching assignments must often be altered to accommodate the exchange. For example, during my exchange an NMSU colleague completed my administrative duties, and a 12-credit load was assigned to Clive McGee. His New Zealand administrative load was assumed by a colleague; I taught undergraduate courses and supervised elementary student teachers.

Benefits of the Experience

The benefits of the experience were many. Professionally I valued my time to reflect. Because I left office politics and committee work behind, I had time to write, to plan lessons, and to observe students and teachers. A typical Hamilton Teachers College day always included morning and afternoon tea. At 10 a.m. and 3 p.m., work stopped for faculty and staff, and 30 minutes of conversation began. Everyone adjourned to a spacious, carpeted room with comfortable chairs and couches grouped around tables. I particularly noted the interchange between faculty and staff. People did not have assigned seats. The college employed a person to make coffee and tea, set out snacks, and clean up the room.

Department faculty meetings were held once a month during a working lunch. My input was sought, and I was made to feel welcome.

Faculty teams often met to discuss course content and to check for interrater reliability on graded assignments. My grading of student papers became more rigorous because A's were truly earned by teacher education students. In the course of the year, students completed a number of written assignments. The content of each assignment and the grading criteria were determined by the faculty teaching the course. Papers were graded by faculty and outside markers. Each marker chose an example of an A, an A-, a B+, a B, a B-, a C+, a C, a C-, a D, and an F paper, and exchanged them with other markers. I truly examined my grading assumptions and my assigned papers carefully. There was indeed a range of performance on the papers.

Assignments

Many of my days were spent observing practice teachers. This was a pleasant task once I mastered driving the college's cars (with standard transmission) on the other side of the road. Primary schools are composed of modular (portable) classrooms that open to a courtyard. Teachers can easily move their classes outside, and parents can comfortably meet with teachers before, during, and after school.

Practice teachers in New Zealand complete three intensive practice-teaching sessions, one each year. During the first experience they observe, conduct lessons with small groups, and keep a personal diary. The diary contains events of interest, challenges they have encountered, characteristics of children, questions about ideas and issues, reflective ideas, and useful hints on teaching. Also during the first experience, practice teachers complete a series of structured tasks on such topics as (a) becoming familiar with the classroom, (b) teacher skills, (c) involvement with children, (d) definitions of teaching and learning, and (e) classroom routines. The second and third sessions involve the students in more rigorous reflection, self-analysis, and guided practice. University observers spend considerable time observing and conferring with practice teachers and their cooperating teachers.

When I was not observing practice teachers, I was teaching sections of courses required of all students: Introduction to Teaching (a first-year course), Curriculum Processes (a second-year course), and Realities of Teaching (a third-year course). Introduction to Teaching includes such topics as description of management behaviors, past observations of teaching behaviors, variation techniques, lesson planning and teaching, teaching and shared evaluation, and planning for difficult management styles. Curriculum Processes builds upon the introductory course, calling for students to conduct an in-depth interview with an influential New Zealand educator, to discuss unintended learning outcomes, to scrutinize their own curriculum beliefs, and to contrast their beliefs with those of teachers and school board members. In Realities of Teaching, students listen to panels of first-year teachers, experienced teachers, and administrators talking about significant issues. They prepare their vitae and practice interpersonal skills and job interviews.

Learnings About Another Culture

I learned more about multicultural issues as I explored the Maori culture. The myths indicate that thousands of years ago Polynesians from Hawaii set sail in large canoes and discovered Aoteraroa, the "Land of the Long White Cloud." The first European to see New Zealand, Abel Tasman, arrived in 1642. The indigenous peoples united under the name Maori, which means ordinary. The Maoris today work hard to preserve their language, heritage, and art. They represent about 12% of the population. New Zealand is proud of its bicultural society. Newcomers to Hamilton Teachers College are welcomed in a *powfiri*, a formal ceremony with speeches in Maori and English. The ceremony concludes with a tour of the campus *marae* (sacred meeting place) and refreshments in the meeting room.

Personal Side of the Experience

Personally, my family and I had a sensational time. We spent our weekends touring the spectacular New Zealand countryside and entertaining and being entertained royally by our Kiwi friends. My nine-year-old daughter was quickly accepted by the 30 children in her Standard 3 class, and my husband obtained a work permit to "relieve" (substitute) in secondary classrooms.

SUGGESTIONS FOR OTHERS SETTING UP EXCHANGES

Because my exchange was such a success, I would like to see other academics participate. The following suggestions may make exchanges easier to accomplish:

1. Work with the college or department faculty to draft the rules and the regulations of the exchange. The material of the National Faculty Exchange (4656 West Jefferson, Suite 140, Fort Wayne, IN 46804) can easily be adapted to meet a college or university's needs. Proceed through the college or university's chain of command to make certain that the program is approved.
2. Decide how many exchanges will be permitted (e.g., one per semester) and how faculty will be chosen (e.g., seniority or match of subject field).
3. Solve the financial concerns (e.g., airfare, salary, and payment of utilities).
4. Investigate visa and insurance issues. Some countries require a visa, and some higher education insurance packages permit the faculty member to add on coverage for an international assignment.
5. Plan welcoming activities for the incoming faculty member, and keep in touch with this colleague abroad. Internet computer capabilities permit daily electronic-mail connections.

6. Use the incoming faculty member's expertise in classes and community functions.
7. Invite the returning colleague to share new ideas and curriculum development insights with faculty.

CONCLUSION

Faculty exchanges contribute directly to helping faculty and students prepare for an increasingly more complicated world order. The faculty members expand their world views and provide more multicultural approaches in their classrooms. Frequently these faculty members arrange exchanges for their colleagues and construct international student teaching programs. They become involved in hosting international visitors and in writing proposals for grants in the international arena. They are in the forefront of productive change.

The Liaison Group for International Educational Exchange (1989) recommends teacher exchanges at all levels because "we cannot expect to reach agreement on solutions to global problems, let alone make serious national commitments to such solutions, without a common international base of knowledge about them" (p. 6).

Exchanges are truly valuable and relatively easy to arrange. They can be built upon contacts that already exist at one's college or university, or the person taking the initiative can spin the globe, choose an area, and find some colleagues to help him or her arrange an exchange.

REFERENCES

Burn, B. B. (1988, Fall). International exchanges and curricular change. *Forum*, pp. 31–34.

Cole, A. L., & Knowles, G. (1992, April). *Extending boundaries: Narratives on exchange*. Paper presented at the Annual Meeting of the American Educational Research Association, San Francisco.

Liaison Group for International Educational Exchange. (1989). *Exchange 2000: International leadership for the next century*. Washington, DC: Author. (Now the Alliance for International Educational and Cultural Exchange, 1090 Vermont Avenue, N.W., Suite 720, Washington, DC 20005.)

Mossberg, B. C. (1990, May 30). College must encourage and reward international exchanges. *Chronicle of Higher Education*, p. 44.

5

EGYPT, METAPHORS, AND ALTERNATIVE PERSPECTIVES

Linda G. Lambert and Morgan Dale Lambert

Why is living in Egypt for two years like a synectics lesson? How does that experience help to build a global perspective?

Teacher educators who have used the powerful teaching strategy called synectics know how effectively it facilitates creative thinking and develops the ability to gain alternative perspectives on problems, issues, and values. The same kind of shift was one of the unexpected results of the experience that the two of us had in living in a dramatically different culture: a fresh view of our own culture, a new frame for our global perspective, and an altered set of metaphors to enrich our thinking and our teaching. That is what we describe in this chapter.

In the synectics strategy the teacher uses metaphor to create distance from a familiar idea or way of thinking: "When you think about school, what kind of machine (or animal or vegetable) comes to mind?" In the instructional activities that follow in the synectics lesson, the learner is guided in experiencing a new perspective and then in reentering more familiar reality from the distant world of imagining.

Our familiar reality was disturbed in spring 1989 when Linda received a telephone invitation to apply for a two-year assignment as a staff development specialist in a curriculum reform project funded by the United States Agency for International Development (USAID). Her role would be to train and assist Egyptian educators in their efforts to revise and modernize their national school curriculum, and to devise strategies for orienting and training the many thousands of classroom teachers to use the new curriculum materials effectively. Although neither of us had ever lived for an extended period in a different country, the decision was surprisingly easy to make. We loved to travel; professionally each of us was ready for a change; and the work seemed as though it might provide something close to the educational equivalent of the Peace Corps experience that we both regretted having passed up earlier in our lives. The time and the place appeared to be right, so we secured leaves and flew off to taste a totally unfamiliar slice of life.

THE EXPERIENCE IN EGYPT

If we had been asked to describe our mental imagery at that stage of our synectic-like experience, our pictures of Egypt probably would have included the Sphinx and the Giza pyramids, scenes of grinding poverty in urban Cairo, teeming thousands in the narrow alleys of exotic bazaars, and perhaps more fanciful views of sailing on the Nile with Elizabeth (Cleopatra) Taylor and Richard (Antony) Burton. Those images were only slightly dimmed by minor anxieties about living and working conditions, interesting employment for Morgan, the challenge of a language barrier, and possible culture shock (as well as reverse culture shock on our return home).

Whatever culture shock we actually experienced never seemed to be of high voltage—more like a mild tingle that intrigues more than it hurts. The press of 15 million people living in close quarters, a traffic pattern that seemed at first to have no pattern, a cacophony of street sounds, a few minor intestinal bouts, dirt and rubble everywhere (even in affluent neighborhoods), children and desperately poor people begging on the streets (but fewer than we expected, certainly fewer than in downtown San Francisco), the exuberance of a people who like each other, a language that sounded more like music than speech, verbal imagery and evocative metaphors, and eventually a war viewed through another's window—all bombarded our senses and heightened our awareness that we were "no longer in Kansas, Dorothy."

Living abroad is indeed an immersing synectics experience that can alter the way in which one sees things, thinks about them, and expresses the thoughts in language. At first we did not realize how different the root metaphors were: family, love, democracy, poverty, education, information, choice, cooperation, men and women. All of them carried new meanings for us as newcomers. It took us a while to realize that our own knowledge base and experience did not transfer laterally and literally. The effect was to create both mental and physical distance from both sets of metaphors, causing us to entertain multiple meanings and remain open for still others. The experience threw into question just who we were: Were we not in a sense the composite drawing of our own metaphors?

The word *family* represents one of those root metaphors or values that have different meanings in our two cultures. Some of our Egyptian friends showed surprise when we talked about traveling back home to visit family. They said, "Forgive us, but we thought that Americans didn't care about family" and "You Americans don't love each other; otherwise why would you let your son or daughter move out of your home?"

Families in Egypt are close from birth to death; they take care of one another. Crime is minimal, partly because bringing shame on the family is the ultimate crime. Homelessness is rarely encountered unless family members have died; mental illness is rare. For devout Moslems, giving to those in need is more than a ritual. We came to respect both the Moslems and the Coptic Christians whom we knew as genuinely devoted to their concepts of living a good life. Their extended family extends the safety net that our welfare state attempts to provide. However, their safety net seems to bind them closer together, whereas our safety net tends to lessen our interdependence.

The readiness of many Egyptians to extend that safety net of friendship and support to include us quickly relieved our anxiety about whether we would be seen as unwelcome intruders. In all of our travels we have never encountered a people who were as warm and as open as the Egyptians were in widening family boundaries to accept us. This was true not only of our work colleagues but of strangers on the streets of Cairo and in the rural villages that we visited in upper Egypt, in the Sinai, and on the Mediterranean coast.

The openness did not usually extend to access to information, however. In an emerging democracy like Egypt, information is erratically defined and reluctantly provided. Access to reasonably accurate and consistent information was one of the staples that we missed most. It was impossible to predict or plan based on solid information, and it was difficult to think critically about the political and social issues without clear and reliable information from multiple sources. Information in Egypt represents the power of the revered hierarchy and has historically been withheld from people outside the ruling elite.

Morgan found a part-time job as a journalist for an English-language weekly newspaper, the *Middle East Times* (MET). One of his most frustrating but amusing exploits as "investigative reporter" was trying to obtain simple facts about a government project that was ostensibly aimed at promoting more efficient use of information. After maneuvering through two lines of armed guards, flashing his MET press card, he was referred to four functionaries. The best response that Morgan received from any of them was a vague assurance from the person in charge, "I will check with my superiors and telephone you." Of course, he never did. The MET assumed a fairly cautious editorial stance, but periodically had news items and whole issues censored. The newspaper itself was banned for a short period soon after we returned home. In contrast, the relative freedom of the American press seemed like a breath of fresh air.

Language fluency is another concept that takes varied forms in different cultures, and it represents a context in which both of us had some very humbling experiences. Most were associated with our personal efforts to learn conversational Arabic, but some were broader revelations of the disadvantages of growing up in a culture that places little value on learning foreign languages. Cairenes are in many ways more cosmopolitan than Americans. When we stopped on the streets to ask for information, it was not unusual to hear the person respond with "Francais?" or "Deutsch?" or "Italiano?" We would have to reply, "Sorry, English only" and then rush back to study our Arabic book. To their credit the Egyptians put up with our linguistic ignorance. Although many Egyptians form stereotypes very quickly, they are playfully tolerant of the enormous diversity that they encounter in their crossroads metropolis Cairo; their stereotyping is not accompanied by the anger or the resentment that often engulfs prejudices in our own country.

The contrast between our two cultures in the way in which we offer and define the concept of choice is also intriguing. Under the press of multiple authorities (religion, government, family, and other hierarchies), the ordinary Egyptian has little margin for making choices. The secondary school student, for example, has a prescribed and common curriculum with only two or three branches—sciences, math, and arts. Fact-oriented national examinations function as mechanistic gateways into technical or academic schools and later into university faculties. There is a readiness and even an impatience among elements of a (Western-educated) intellectual elite to jump quickly into radical reform, shifting the emphasis to modern problem-solving and critical-thinking forms of education in which choice and decision making are invaluable skills. However, the hurdles are high and the resistance from traditionalism is powerful. We were both involved in a research-and-development effort to design and implement a significantly different secondary school system, a Secondary School System of Credit and Choice, but before it had a chance to get off the ground, critics were assailing the "choice plan" as a dangerous "Western" (American) idea that threatened Islam and tradition. The impression that America is infatuated with choice is understandable, but misleading when applied outside the realm of business (witness the passionate divisions over choice in schooling and abortion).

Education in Egypt has traditionally been perceived as acquisition and recitation of information. For many Egyptian children that means fragmented information, never to be ground into knowledge. Teachers are poorly trained, earn about $30.00 a month, and often teach in small classrooms with 50–75 children. Yet many of the teachers whom Linda encountered in staff development sessions were curious, ready to learn new ideas and instructional techniques, and eager to transfer the ideas and the techniques into their classes. Morgan found the students in the Teaching Certificate Program that he designed for the American University in Cairo to be generally open to innovative ideas and practices. After two years of working with her Egyptian colleagues, Linda felt the satisfaction of knowing that the tell-and-test model was gradually being challenged and replaced by better-designed curriculum and instruction inviting children to be active learners who work together cooperatively. (Cooperation itself is a valued goal for Egyptians, but cooperation of the narrow and inflexible kind.)

These new instructional goals are part of a national education reform effort in Egypt that was initiated by a man who was minister of education when we arrived. He is now the speaker of the People's Assembly, but still very influential in the education arena. Clearly the winds of educational change are blowing in Egypt, but they are notoriously changeable, and the desert is vast. We are watching anxiously and hopefully to see if they will produce any lasting change in the educational and cultural contours of this ancient land.

The pace of change and the concept of time itself seemed very different in Egypt. Living in another culture brings with it an altered perspective on time: Daily body rhythms are different, not accentuated by frequent changes in activities. Time with each other moves like a dance, not pulled at by undone tasks or incomplete lists; one goes to sleep when one is sleepy, wakes up when one is not sleepy anymore. Change takes hundreds of years and emerges naturally from the ebb and flow of human activity, not to be defined by moments or events. The 5,000-year-old temple walls depict the same human dilemmas with which we still struggle. However, severe problems are now bombarding the people of Egypt and the Third World generally that do not seem to respond to the historical ways: population growth, pollution, ethnic rivalries, scarce natural resources, depleted soil, a new kind of poverty (inner-city poverty relying on a market economy), and an entrenched bureaucracy that resists and coopts change efforts.

This description of our perspective-altering experiences in Egypt would of course be incomplete without referring to the Gulf War (perhaps the ultimate form of synectics experience). Despite our proximity to the battle zone, we felt quite safe—once it became clear that the Scud missiles could not reach Cairo. To begin with, none of our Egyptian friends and acquaintances believed that there would actually be a hot war ("They'll all wave their swords wildly and then make a deal"); the concepts of an ultimatum that had sharp teeth and a deadline that was real seemed almost incomprehensible. When the fighting actually started, the bulk of our friends grudgingly backed President Hosni Mubarak's decision to support United Nations actions, were confident that the Western forces were invincible, were saddened by the slaughter of Iraqi soldiers and civilians, and were surprised only by the decision to call a halt before Saddam Hussein was eliminated. A relatively small but growing minority (labeled extremists and fundamentalists in the government-controlled press) identified with Saddam's attempt to cast himself as a reincarnation of the universal Arab hero, Saladin, who had defeated the Crusaders in key battles. However, once the war was over, most Egyptians seemed quite willing to forgive and forget; after all, Saddam had made "just one mistake."

REENTRY

One of the minor anxieties that we felt as we went to Egypt was what we would experience when we returned—perhaps a reverse form of culture shock. Indeed, reentry took time and required patience, but it was not truly difficult for us. Most of the adjustments were pleasant and comforting: relative order, comparative cleanliness, reasonable dependability in the service industry, a wide array of products in supermarkets, prices that were high but "fixed," and freedom to question, to seek information, to criticize authority openly. However, there were many things that we missed: a chauffeur to take us to work, an evening at the opera house and a fine restaurant for $10.00, a garage attendant who washed our car daily, a young boy who came to the apartment to pick up and deliver our ironing, and social access to national leaders in art and diplomacy as well as education. As we passed the six-month hurdle of being returnees, we were conscious of a vague ennui, a sense of Is this all there is to being back?, an itch to do more traveling in exotic places.

Linda's reabsorption into her professional life was all too quick (resuming her teaching and taking on the responsibilities of department chair left her little time for reentry anxiety). Although she had learned enough Arabic to converse simply and to understand the gist of meetings with her Egyptian colleagues, she experienced newfound wonder in once more being able to teach and discuss ideas in her own language—especially in terms of deciphering complex ideas and discovering new meanings and nuances. Morgan's readjustment took longer because he decided not to seek another superintendency, but to build a new career as an educational consultant. Both of us have ambivalent feelings about changes in our profession that occurred during our absence, especially the current enthusiasm about restructuring: on the one hand, great satisfaction that some of the goals and the values toward which we worked over many years are finally receiving the recognition that they deserve; on the other hand, a desire that we could have been involved during two critical years of action, and impatience to resume leadership roles.

We have naturally been alert to the changing of metaphors that comes with new language experience. On our return we heard new words and phrases for the first time (or at least for the first time in the new context or usage): *Latina/Latino; full inclusion; rap; political correctness; downsizing the workforce; women of color; confirmation conversion; Willie Horton–esque; shifting dependency ratio.* Are these just euphemisms, or do they represent changing root metaphors?

Linda recently became embroiled in a heated argument with a group of feminists about alterations in the role of women. They claimed that nothing truly important had changed, whereas we are sure that we have observed a number of dramatic changes. From the presidency of the National Press Club, to prized overseas journalistic assignments, to top positions in organizations, to breaking the gender line in the US Senate club, more women have been moving into positions of power. Although the beautiful body has not entirely abandoned the new car in the TV ads, media in all forms are finally leaving behind the little-girl image of womanhood. Are these perceptions accurate, or do the changes seem more dramatic to us because we see them juxtaposed to a Middle Eastern culture in which women are still considered to be another species, less intelligent and able, highly volatile, and less credible in their perceptions of the world? Even in Egypt there was evidence of movement away from cultural captivity toward equal access to higher education and increased opportunity for professional employment and leadership/management positions (the director of the curriculum development center where Linda did her consulting was a highly respected woman).

ALTERED AGENDAS

How has the synectical experience of living in a foreign culture for two years affected us? The most dramatic change has been a vividly heightened awareness of our values and agendas for action:

- We are more patient with change—but also more dedicated to it.

- Our social activist agenda is sharper in focus and more determined: "Third World" communities within our own country; the role of women and ethnic minorities; democracy (particularly the roles of choice and information); and the Democratic party (now unexpectedly in power but still in need of radical reform).
- We are more impatient with those who have much but complain if their affluence or comfort is threatened.
- We value our family more than ever.

We highly recommend an experience like ours to any educator. We had perceived ourselves to be open, globally aware, involved individuals. Yet immersion in a foreign culture for an extended period gave us distance and perspective that helped us see our own culture and the broader world with infinitely greater clarity and depth.

POSTSCRIPT

In summer 1993, Linda was invited to return to Egypt for six weeks. Cautioned about the growing tide of fundamentalism, she weighed the risks and the opportunities. Eventually she could not resist the pull of Egypt and friends, and the tantalizing chance to assess the progress of the curriculum development center since its inception, to retrain staff, and to help write the work plan for the next year.

The winds of change have continued to blow adversely since we left Egypt: more women wearing the veil; almost no Americans in sight on the streets of Cairo; persistent government paranoia about attacks on foreigners; and strident anti-Western editorials, even in the government-controlled press. Some of the winds have been buffeting the center and its fragile reform initiatives:

- Several editorials in an opposition paper targeting Linda by name, linking her and the center to a "Western plot to destroy Islam"
- Wavering support for the center's work from the minister of education
- Withdrawal of three primary-grade environmental education textbooks, probably the best products of early center collaboration
- Strong indications that USAID priorities have shifted worldwide and that financial support for basic education in Egypt will soon end.

The future of the center is not the largest concern in Egypt now: Greater concerns focus on the future of a fledgling democracy (and the Mubarak government), early efforts at a market economy, and the reversal in movements to liberate women. Linda's return to Egypt after two years added even richer perspectives to our synectics experience, casting the future of education and the future of democracy into the same, complex metaphor—in both Egypt and the United States.

6

PREPARATION OF INSERVICE TEACHERS FOR AN INTERNATIONAL STUDY EXPERIENCE: A CASE STUDY

Patricia Betts Roach

The excitement of a study trip abroad sends our spirits soaring and releases our fantasies of taking the perfect trip to the perfect land to visit the perfect people. Of course, we are the perfect travelers: We know how to say hello, thank you, and goodbye; we know the major cultural taboos; and we take no cultural bias or ethnocentric behaviors or personal problems with us. Although someone who has traveled to this country has warned us of flies, heat, unsafe water, and expected health problems, these things are too unimportant to worry about.

- "Have you applied for your passport?"/"Yes, and you should see my pictures; they are awful!"
- "I've never flown."/"Don't worry—it's fun!"
- "Wow! We are really going to India—for six weeks!"

The purpose of the study trip abroad was to provide an opportunity for teachers to enhance their global perspective through experiencing a culture very different from their own. The study trip enabled classroom teachers to spend six weeks in India: two weeks of intensive classroom study conducted by Indian university professors and four weeks of travel and study throughout India.

To ensure that the teachers were ready for the experience, project staff gave much thought to the preparation phase. They designed the overall orientation to add to the knowledge that the teachers already had about India and to provide an opportunity for the teachers to consider their own attitudes and values about diversity and common human interests. In addition, project staff shared information about the group's living and traveling agenda.

PREPARATION FOR THE ORIENTATION

Initially, project staff carefully analyzed the credentials of the 11 teachers who would travel. They consisted of 10 females and 1 male, with an age range from 26 to 50. They represented rural, urban, and suburban schools, both elementary and secondary, and a variety of subjects, including English, art, and social studies as well as the total elementary school curriculum. Approximately half held master's degrees.

Project staff were also interested in the travel experience of the group. One teacher had traveled and lived in South America for a year, another teacher had grown up in India, and a third teacher had traveled out of the country on a two-week tour. Eight teachers had not traveled to any degree; in fact, this would be the first airplane trip for four of them.

To prepare for the academic portion of the orientation, the curriculum director conducted several surveys, one to determine specific information about India in the textbooks being used by Arkansas teachers, one to determine the amount of curriculum time devoted to the study of India, and one to find out from 1,000 students what they wanted to know about India.

In anticipation of the trip and as part of the proposal-writing process to receive funding, the teachers completed assigned readings and participated in several days of inservice activities related to contemporary India. As a result of their studies, the teachers chose specific topics for study while in India: India as a national and international marketplace, democracy in India, the educational process, and art as cultural expression.

During the spring before the summer travel, the project director traveled to India to make arrangements with Loyola College in Madras to provide professors for the two-week intensive-study portion of the trip. In addition, he visited hotels where the group would be staying and made slides to use in the orientation.

THE ORIENTATION PROCESS

After analysis of the academic and travel experience of the participants, examination of the Loyola lecture schedule, and consideration of time and budget constraints, the codirectors decided that the orientation would consist of two eight-hour days with emphasis on four areas: a broad historical and social framework to ensure perspective, social and emotional aspects of travel, an overview of the curriculum task to be completed in India, and immediate concerns. Because the group had worked together on other projects for approximately two to three years, all of the participants knew one another well, with the exception of one newcomer; therefore the usual get-acquainted activities were not required.

Much thought was given to who should conduct the academic orientation. A college professor with a national reputation was chosen because of his expertise in Indian social history and his reputation for telling "wonderful stories." His writings were on the group's required reading list. His sessions were short, related to specific places that the teachers would visit, and basically cultural rather than political in nature. He was assisted by an Indian art historian, who provided slides and commentary on famous works of art that the teachers would experience, and emphasized the historical and social importance of the art to the Indian people. Approximately eight hours, interspersed with Indian foods, Indian music, and slides, were used for academic orientation.

The second phase of the orientation, approximately four hours, dealt with social and emotional aspects of the trip. A high school counselor with whom the teachers were already familiar provided activities to enhance their ability to observe and to practice objectivity. He emphasized the commonalities of group members as well as the commonalities of people in general. Also, he provided activities to enhance group solidarity and spoke to the group about culture shock and the difficulties to be expected from rooming together for six weeks.

The third phase of the orientation focused on the curriculum tasks to be completed in India. The curriculum director reported the findings of the surveys that had been conducted, identified a framework for the tasks, and with input from the participants established a time frame for the completion of all the major tasks. Because most of these decisions had been made during the writing of the proposal, only one hour was devoted to the tasks during orientation.

Approximately three hours were scheduled for the fourth phase of the orientation, immediate concerns. Thirty-minute segments were devoted to health issues, living conditions, and general how-to information. In addition, these issues were discussed at a social gathering during the evening and during meal and coffee breaks. The project director, who had just returned from India, directed these sessions. He showed slides; discussed hotels, meals, laundry, travel, and currency; and answered hundreds of questions.

All persons conducting the orientation session except the counselor had personally lived or studied in India. The historian had spent his academic life studying in India for a year or so at a time. The art historian was Indian by birth, had studied at a Canadian university, and was currently living in the United States. The project director had traveled and studied in India five times over 20 years. The curriculum director had studied in India twice in that time period and had traveled there as part of an inservice teacher group very similar to this one.

Although the participants entered into all the activities enthusiastically, their major interest was in immediate and personal matters, such as what they should take to wear, whether they would be able to use their hair dryers, what the food would be like, how their families could get in touch with them, whether they should take toilet paper, how many rolls of film they would need, whether others were going to take malaria tablets, whether others had had their cholera shots yet, how much the cholera shot would cost, and how much money they should take. The codirectors of the project discussed answers with the group as well as with participants individually. Two of the participants did not attend the orientation session; one was sick and the other was teaching summer school. Many phone calls and letters were required to ensure that these teachers had information about immediate concerns. Unfortunately both of them were inexperienced travelers.

No formal evaluation of the orientation was conducted. The codirectors believed that because of the cohesive nature of the group, the time already spent in the study of India, and the many opportunities for individual questions and small group discussions, most of the questions had been answered. They decided that an evaluation would be more meaningful after the group returned.

REALIZATIONS WITH HINDSIGHT

Looking back, project staff realized that most of the orientation—13 of the 16 hours—had dealt with what we identified as future needs. Moreover, the immediate concerns to which we devoted the remaining 3 hours were in fact future needs to many participants. Almost any issue other than items to take, immunizations to obtain, tickets, and arrival time at the airport was treated by participants as a future need. As a result, teachers responded to what we thought were immediate, serious concerns with off-handed comments such as the following:

- "I've already talked to my doctor and he told me that if I would . . . , I would have no problems."
- "I know conditions are not going to be like those here, but we camp out a lot, so I can live anywhere for six weeks."

- "Actually, I'm very healthy."
- "I'm really a very strong person emotionally; I don't think I'll have any trouble with culture shock. After all, I have been studying about India and getting ready for this trip for almost three years."
- "No, I don't think this group will have any trouble getting along. We have been working together on various projects for about three years."

As a result of the difference between project staff and teachers about immediate versus future needs, issues that we thought had been covered and understood in the orientation session and problems that we had not even considered began to surface almost immediately. In fact, the first problem arose at the airport in London when one teacher who was fearful that she would be left behind insisted that we had not properly prepared them for the experience because we had not told them what to do if they became separated from the group. Another concern was airport security and customs. One member of the group felt discriminated against because her bags had been opened and the bags of other group members had not been. We also soon realized that the nontravelers (approximately half of the group) did not know how to read their airline tickets, use airport monitors to obtain gate information, or find departure gates. Project staff were focused on India and the India experience, whereas many of the travelers, especially those who were inexperienced, were more concerned about the travel itself.

LESSONS ALONG THE WAY

What did we learn about the orientation process as the trip progressed? First and most important, we learned that the teachers did not remember many of the matters that had been discussed or did not believe certain cautions to be valid. An example is the emphasis that was placed on the health dangers of drinking the water, of eating fresh fruits and vegetables that had been peeled using the water, and of using ice cubes. Although all the participants used bottled water, almost all consistently ate fresh fruits and vegetables from the buffets in "nice" hotels. We found this to be true of the persons who had previously traveled as well as the inexperienced travelers. One teacher said that the bartender had told her that the ice in the hotel was safe. Another teacher summed it up this way: "I'm sure in a nice hotel like this, the food is safe." Consequently a constant problem was stomach disorders.

Statistics kept during the two weeks of the academic session indicated that the number of lectures attended (of a possible 19) ranged from 100% (by three teachers, all of whom had previous travel experience) to 47% (by a person who had never even flown or traveled in the United States). Despite the stomach disorders, the majority of the teachers participated at a very high rate; the average attendance across all lectures was 84%. This rate reflected many visits to hotel doctors and local chemist shops and a strong sense of determination on the part of the participants. Moreover, although the rate of attendance was satisfactory, the quality of the experience and the extension of experiences that could have been available were limited by illness.

Second, we learned that the orientation session did not anticipate the special needs of those who were completely inexperienced travelers. In many ways the travel process itself took on monumental proportions, actually keeping the inexperienced travelers from gaining a real experience of India. For several of them, traveling and dealing with the group were emotionally overwhelming and seemed to add an additional level to the culture shock experienced by most of the teachers.

Third, the complexities of group travel are very difficult to explain. Culture shock causes people to act and react differently than they themselves can imagine. Although this phenomenon was discussed in detail in the orientation session, discord within the group came as a surprise to many. Because the group members had known one another for several years, this was especially disappointing for some. Although minor conflicts were evident several times during the six weeks, conflict between two persons in particular was continual and occasionally disruptive to the whole group. Another person disassociated herself from the group.

Although the social and emotional aspects of the orientation session proved to be less successful than expected, the academic part provided a strong framework that was evident in the questioning by participants during the lectures. The majority of the teachers showed genuine curiosity and interest in all matters Indian. The curriculum task moved along as planned in the orientation session. Teachers gathered materials as part of their wider experiences and wrote lesson plans to reflect contemporary India. As a result, all of the curriculum plans based on Indian newspaper articles, magazines, textbooks, and a variety of first-hand experiences were completed before the return home. The primary criterion used to judge the materials was the question, "Could we have written this lesson plan if we had not traveled to India?" If the answer was yes, the plan was replaced with another.

Finally, we learned that the difficulty of preparing people for international group travel is much more complex than we had imagined. In the beginning we felt very confident about the orientation that we had planned and initiated. After the trip we were less sure. Approximately 60 days after the group had arrived back in Arkansas and life was beginning to return to normal for most of the participants, the codirectors prepared an open-ended questionnaire to identify participants' perceptions of the adequacy of the orientation. When asked, "How well did the orientation prepare you for the India experience?", the participants focused all but two comments on traveling or health issues rather than on preparation for experiencing another culture. Comments included the following:

- "Practical points of traveling should have been more detailed."
- "[We] should have been warned about long waits at airports."
- "[We] should have been warned about the problems associated with drinking the water."
- "[We] should have been made aware that stomach/intestinal problems are 'almost guaranteed.'"
- "Food problems should have been discussed at length."
- "Medicine and health problems in India should have been discussed."
- "[There should have been] more emphasis on the health aspect of going to India/a list of foods and situations to avoid."
- "Had I known what I know now, I would have left all my shoes and clothes at home and brought only food."

All of the points made in these comments had been carefully covered in the orientation session. Therefore the question that really needs to be addressed is how the orientation session can be planned in such a way that these concerns will impress participants without being overstated. How can the physical, emotional, and psychological health of the participants be more realistically addressed?

CONCLUSION

To travel and to experience another culture first-hand seems to be an important step in attaining a global perspective; however, to experience a vastly different culture promotes insecurities and fears in the individual that may limit rather than enhance growth. What is the process by which one begins to attain a global perspective? How important is it that an orientation be planned to minimize personal concerns and maximize a global experience? What criteria should be used to choose members of a group? As the issue of global perspective is debated, consideration must also be given to the process and the practicality of attainment. If study trips abroad are considered to be an important part of the process, more needs to be understood about preparing teachers and students so that they are physically, socially, and psychologically ready for the experience. Literature on most of these issues is nonexistent. Additional case studies are essential.

7
STUDY OF WORLD HISTORY IN A MULTIETHNIC CLASSROOM
Diane Sudbury

I sat at my desk one day wondering how to bridge the gap between the life of a seventh-grade student and the subject of world history. Somehow I was reminded of the Grand Canyon. Undaunted, I proceeded to review several teaching strategies that might enable at least a skydiver's glide across the enormous gorge of pubescent disinterest in world history. My goal was to have my students arrive at the other side feeling informed and inspired. Ultimately, many students arrived safe and sound, a few others landed on the steep precipices right below the opposite edge, while still others plummeted to the river below. However, my metaphor puts me ahead of myself.

I am fortunate to teach world history in a classroom that is a true microcosm of the world. My students are ethnically diverse, and many of them have expressed a genuine curiosity about their roots and heritage. As we began our study of the Middle Ages, I sought ways to expand the European perspective to include viewpoints and attitudes from Africa, China, and Japan. The students' enthusiasm and curiosity resulted in my offering a variety of explorations from which they could choose to study areas of the world and subjects in which they were truly interested.

TOPICS AND PROCEDURES

The exploratory topics that I offered to the students were Africa/Asia (China, Japan) in the Middle Ages; Art in the Middle Ages and the Renaissance; Knighthood; Unicorns and the Bayeux Tapestry; Weaponry; and Medicine, Dentistry, and Other Forms of Torture During the Middle Ages. Through these explorations, students compared and contrasted African leaders such as Sunni Ali and Mansa Musa with Kublai Khan, the Tokugawa rulers, and Confucius. They likened medieval European knights to Japanese samurai, exploring the armor and the codes of each. They studied the paintings of Michelangelo and Leonardo da Vinci along with the scroll art of Yen Li-Pen and the Benin sculptures that honored the African kings between 1400 and 1600. They investigated the architecture of European castles and cathedrals alongside that of the Japanese Himeji castle and the Al-Azhar University in Africa.

I placed pictures of these noted people and places on my bulletin boards at the beginning of the year. None were labeled. The only identification was a number and questions above the pictures that asked, What culture? What time? At the start of the year, the students could only guess what the pictures represented. By the end of their explorations, they were familiar with most of the pictures.

Each of the topics came with a set of procedures for exploring it. I wanted the students to be involved in and use as many modalities for learning as possible, so most of the directions for the various explorations involved research, writing, artwork, cooperative learning, and presentation.

Groups formed around areas of interest. As soon as all the students in a particular interest group had completed individual research on their topic, they could meet and share what they had learned with one another. Each topic had a set of questions as well as activities associated with it, so students helped each other answer the questions more completely by sharing information. In this way each of the groups became "expert" on many different aspects of the Middle Ages. The culminating activity to these explorations was to have the expert groups present what they had learned to the rest of the class. Because each topic had artwork as part of the exploration, all groups had visuals to accompany their presentations.

Art in the Middle Ages and the Renaissance: An Illustration

To explain this process further, I would like to detail the exploration activities for Art in the Middle Ages and the Renaissance. I had two world history classes this year. Each of the classes consisted of students at various academic and ability levels. The activities were designed with the idea that all students could be successful at their own level. In these two classes I had many students who had expressed an interest in drawing and creating. (Evidence of their interest could often be observed on desks and bathroom walls throughout the school). Many of these students therefore chose to investigate Art in the Middle Ages and the Renaissance. Once they chose their topic , I handed them instructions like these:

Art in the Middle Ages and the Renaissance

1. Who was Emperor Hui Tsung? How did his painting affect his ability to rule? Investigate this famous ruler.
2. Present your information to the class along with an example of his work.
3. Compare Emperor Hui Tsung's paintings with those of Michelangelo and da Vinci.
4. Create a sculpture of a Benin queen mother out of playdough. Present your sculpture and research on the Benin sculptures to the class.
5. What surprised you about your exploration of this subject (one page)?
6. Include all colored pictures given to you in your packet.

Once they had their instructions, they were urged to go to the library and check out books that would help them in their research. I also provided my own books for them to explore. I have collected many art and history books from all over the world. I also have some of the latest information on Africa, China, and Japan coming out of the Clio Project in Berkeley. I made all of this available to students during class time. Also, I gave them time in class for their research, and we went to the school library as well. As a result, the students produced some fascinating sculptures and presentations. Several students in both classes attempted to duplicate some of the works of Michelangelo. I now have a collection of clay popes, masks, stallions, and even the Pieta. Many discussions arose after students presented their information to other members of the class.

Another outcome of the art exploration was the observation by many of the students that the paintings from the early Middle Ages were much more primitive than the paintings from the later Middle Ages or the Renaissance. I had several of these paintings up in my classroom, and students used them to point out the differences as well as to compare paintings among cultures.

STUDENTS' RESPONSES

Many of my African-American students chose to explore Africa in the Middle Ages. They approached their study with such interest and pride that at times I had trouble keeping them supplied with information. One of these students took her information home to share with her parents, aunts, and uncles. She often commented to me afterward about additional information that her family would give her once she would share what she knew. This dialogue was an unexpected result of the assignment.

My Asian students were enthusiastic to learn about the Himeji castle and the famous Asian leaders of the period. They also read and discussed some mythology that emanated from medieval Japan and China. They introduced other students to the beauty and the brutality of the samurai, the emperors, and the ruling families. They compared and contrasted the medieval warriors from the Asian countries with the knights of Europe. They learned how to write the Chinese symbols for certain words properly and then demonstrated, step by step, how to construct the symbols. They shared pictures of Asian art, and for fun one group brought fortune cookies to share with their classmates on the day of their presentation.

CULMINATING ARTWORK

No matter what continent or culture the groups explored, each group produced a giant colored illustration from their subject area. This illustration was done by transferring pictures onto a piece of paper with the use of an overhead. Once the enlarged image was displayed on the paper, the students could trace and color the magnified image. The students traced and colored the Himeji castle, a Benin princess, Timbuktu and the Al-Azhar University, and a samurai and a knight, to mention only a few. When they were completed, the pictures were labeled with the name of the culture that they represented. They were then displayed as decorations on the walls of the auditorium where we held our World Cultural Faire and Feast this year. The feelings of pride and satisfaction reflected on the faces of the students as they hung their own pictures on the wall enhanced the enjoyment of this event.

RATIONALE

I had my students do multifaceted explorations to avoid the copy-from-the-encyclopedia syndrome that inevitably results when a teacher asks for a report on historical subjects. Not only did I want them to research subjects; I wanted them to do something with the information—to sculpt, to create, to color, and to talk about the information that they gathered. Finally, I wanted them to share what they had experienced with others. I wanted this shared experience to underscore the fact that the Middle Ages did not take place just in Europe, that art and learning and invention came from all over the world. I wanted them to know that heroic warriors were shoguns and samurai as well as knights. I wanted them to hear about Mansa Musa and Timbuktu as well as Raphael and Rome.

Judging from the passion and the pride that many of the students brought to their personally selected topics, I think that we shared a common glide across that canyon of world history apathy and landed on the side of increased knowledge and understanding of a variety of places and topics in the history of the world during the Middle Ages. I am hopeful that these explorations and the resulting presentations increased the students' interest in, and awareness of, other world cultures. I feel that many of them came away feeling a renewed pride in themselves and their heritage, as well as a new respect for the cultures represented in their classroom.

I sincerely hope that the experiences and the strategies presented to my students and others will increase awareness of the differences and the commonalities among us on this tiny globe. My goal is that such activities increase the consciousness of how gratifying and enriching it can be for both student and teacher to think, teach, and act globally.

8

IMPLEMENTATION OF GLOBAL EDUCATION IN THE CLASSROOM: A COMPARISON OF SWEDISH AND AMERICAN EDUCATORS

Audrey E. Wright

International tensions, the fragile economy, environmental pollution, drugs, disappearing resources, poverty, lawlessness, population problems, medical dilemmas, the collapsing family, and media maladies are the major concerns facing the world in the 1990s, according to Cornish (1990). Unfortunately the trends related to these issues are not likely to disappear in the next century. Because the world is becoming more interdependent, the need to prepare students to deal with these and other issues as we rapidly approach the 21st century is challenging educators everywhere. This is evident in the massive number of articles recently written on global education (Anderson, 1991; Ramler, 1991; Tucker & Cistone, 1991).

The United States has espoused the goals of global education primarily to maintain its position of international strength, militarily and economically. "In today's world, politicians, business leaders, and environmentalists are ill-equipped if they do not understand international political events, global markets, and the interdependence of the global environment" (Bruce, Podenski, & Anderson, 1990, p. 21). The National Governors Association, meeting in New York in December 1987, called a global perspective the "key to prosperity." In 1989 the governors recommended that global, international, and foreign language education become part of basic education for all students.

Other countries, such as Sweden, have been compelled to consider global issues because of their size and geographical location as well as their economic interdependence. Swedish people have long been concerned with environmental issues such as global warming and nuclear fallout, and with the need for students to learn a second language, namely English. Sweden's growing multicultural population, the emergence of the common market, and changes in the former Soviet bloc and Germany have contributed to a growing sense that knowledge and attitudes about cultural diversity and international issues need to be incorporated into the curriculum with greater fervor. The Swedish National Board of Education in its 1989 report, *Action Programme for the Internationalisation of Education,* reemphasized the need to infuse global issues more intensely into the school curriculum. Interviews with educators and the general population in Sweden in 1991 led me to believe that politicians were still very concerned with the degree to which global issues had actually been implemented in their nation's schools.

How prepared are American students for a shrinking planet with escalating social, economic, ecological, and political problems? Although the literature in the United States seems overwhelmingly to support a need for infusing global education into the curriculum, it also seems to question the degree to which global issues are actually being addressed in each district's curriculum. Sweden, on the other hand, is often viewed as a country that is open to diversity and whose people are knowledgeable about global issues, presumably because it has done a better job of addressing both in its schools. Comparing the experiences and the practices of the two countries may be illuminating to the goal of implementing global education in American schools (Altbach, 1989; Tye & Kniep, 1991).

This chapter reports the results of a survey of Swedish and American teachers regarding the teaching of global issues in their classrooms. The objectives of the study were (a) to determine if teachers in Sweden were implementing more of the goals of global education in their classrooms than American teachers were; (b) to identify the areas that seemed to receive the most attention and the least attention from teachers; and (c) to determine how teachers were actually implementing the goals that they claimed to be teaching.

METHOD

The populations selected for the study were teachers from Vaxjo, Sweden, and Warrensburg, Missouri. These two communities were used for several reasons. First, they are of similar size and house universities with teacher education programs. Second, Vaxjo University and Central Missouri State University have international agreements that make it easier to generate the type of cooperation necessary for such a study. Finally, both institutions consider international cooperation and global education to be an important component of their mission, so it might be presumed that the teachers who live in the surrounding areas would be more global in their thinking, having been either directly or indirectly influenced by these institutions.

The questionnaire developed for the study (see Appendix 8-A) was a 22-item Likert scale that focused on the goals most often espoused in the literature on global education. The teachers were asked to respond to each of the items by circling the number corresponding to the statement best describing their circumstance or viewpoint: 4—Taught in my classroom; 3—Should be taught in my classroom but is not now taught; 2—Not taught in my class but in another one in my school; and 1—Should not be taught. They were also asked briefly to describe how they taught four of the items that they claimed to be teaching. The descriptions were seen as a way of substantiating what was actually taking place in the classroom.

The questionnaire was developed to reflect Hanvey's (1976) definition of global education and goals developed by Michigan's Department of Education, the Foreign Policy Association, Hilda Taba (Collins & Zakariya, 1982), and Williams (1988). It was piloted with Swedish teachers attending the International Reading Association congress in Sweden in 1990 and with teachers enrolled in graduate courses at Central Missouri State University in spring 1990. It was later translated into Swedish by Torgney Tarnhuvud, a teacher in the Vaxjo school system, and re-fined by a researcher at Vaxjo University. The Swedish questionnaire was then distributed to all the schools in Vaxjo by the teacher education department of Vaxjo University. Because global education is seen as an area that can be implemented in all subjects and at all grade levels in varying degrees, data were solicited from all the teachers in the school districts involved.

A total of 29 Swedish teachers and 55 American teachers (K–12) responded to the questionnaire. The responses from Swedish teachers were solicited during the last week of school in May; those from American teachers in the fall. This may account in some degree for the fewer responses from Swedish teachers.

FINDINGS

A comparison of the Swedish and American responses by item is provided in Table 8-1. Swedish teachers were significantly more global than American teachers in the following nine areas, in order of significance:

1. Students study the disparities of production, distribution, and consumption of necessities such as food among the countries of the world. (Item 14)
2. Students study how religion impacts on the values and culture of different societies. (Item 20)
3. Students are taught that everyone on earth has the right to an equal share of the earth's resources. (Item 8)
4. Students are taught the benefits as well as the difficulties inherent in a world of cultural diversity. (Item 11)
5. Students are taught that citizen participation in government varies among political systems of the world. (Item 5)
6. Students are taught about the dangers to the ecology of the unlimited growth of population, land use, and energy consumption. (Item 9)
7. Students are taught that individuals, their towns, families, state and country have tangible economic connections with other nations and peoples of the world. (Item 2)
8. Students are taught to inquire into current world issues and analyze them objectively. (Item 17)
9. Students are taught that the earth's inhabitants have a common dependency on the way the planet works. (Item 3)

The four items that were most often identified by both groups as being incorporated into their classrooms included the following, in order of significance:

1. Students are taught that every human being on earth has the inherent right to a sense of self-worth. (Item 4)
2. Students are taught that learning is a lifelong process. (Item 12)
3. Students learn to recognize and accept that everyone's perception of the world is not necessarily the same. (Item 19)
4. Students are taught to be responsible contributors to their present environment and the future global environment. (Item 15)

Both groups seemed most to avoid teaching the following items:

1. Students study the impact of technology on political, social and economic conditions of all the world's inhabitants. (Item 21)
2. Students are taught how to forecast change and design alternative futures. (Item 22)

DESCRIPTORS AND REACTIONS

The information reported in this section was gleaned from written comments made by both groups. The comments were solicited to identify how teachers

TABLE 8-1

GOALS ESPOUSED FOR GLOBAL EDUCATION: AN ITEM-BY-ITEM
COMPARISON OF AMERICAN AND SWEDISH EDUCATORS

Item #	American $N = 55$		Swedish $N = 29$		F Ratio	p
	Mean	SD	Mean	SD		
1	3.38	0.80	3.62	0.93	1.25	.2666
2	2.92	0.86	3.50	1.01	6.25	.0138*
3	3.31	0.93	3.73	0.67	4.40	.0365*
4	3.92	0.20	3.96	0.38	0.34	.5705
5	2.88	1.04	3.58	0.90	8.78	.0042*
6	3.33	0.93	3.65	0.63	2.67	.1021
7	2.95	1.09	3.27	0.83	1.78	.1821
8	2.86	1.12	3.77	0.59	15.25	.0004*
9	3.03	1.05	3.65	0.80	7.21	.0086*
10	3.30	0.99	3.35	0.89	0.03	.8464
11	2.95	1.05	3.65	0.63	10.05	.0025*
12	3.86	0.48	3.85	0.37	0.02	.8747
13	2.93	1.06	3.23	0.91	1.58	.2105
14	2.51	0.98	3.58	0.76	24.06	.0001*
15	3.41	0.92	3.73	0.60	2.59	.1077
16	3.45	0.88	3.31	1.05	0.40	.5335
17	2.91	1.01	3.42	0.99	4.66	.0317*
18	3.24	0.98	3.46	0.86	0.98	.3478
19	3.47	0.85	3.77	0.51	2.70	.1004
20	2.68	0.97	3.62	0.85	17.72	.0002*
21	2.61	1.05	3.23	0.95	6.54	.0120*
22	2.70	1.01	3.08	0.93	2.65	.1037

Note: Items identified in boldface type indicate positive responses from both groups.
*$p < .05$

perceived themselves actually to be implementing the items that they claimed to be teaching. Their examples offer insight to teacher educators whose job is to ensure that teachers are aware of global issues and capable of developing strategies necessary for incorporating them into the curriculum.

American and Swedish teachers most often described how they worked on developing the concept that every human being on earth has the right to a sense of self-worth (Item 4). The descriptors included acceptance of each student and his or her errors, discussions, games, celebration of special days, and reading and writing stories. The majority of descriptors tended to emphasize the modeling of acceptance as the best way to develop each student's self-concept. The train of thought appeared to be that through development of self-concept, a child would accept the value that everyone has the right to a sense of self-worth. Research conducted by educational psychologists has linked a positive self-concept to students' academic success (Harris, 1986). This may explain why both groups correlated so highly in citing the inclusion of this area in their curriculum.

Both groups frequently identified two other goals related to self-worth as being incorporated into their classrooms. However, they seldom described how students learned that human beings have common needs and expressions of emotion (Item 16) and that everyone's perception of the world is not necessarily the same (Item 19). The question therefore remains whether students are truly learning to respect and accept diversity and similarity in the human species or are learning only to value themselves and others like them.

The goal that both groups described second most frequently involved teaching children how to resolve conflict and controversy (Item 1). Examples of methods used included encouraging children to talk out their problems when they experienced conflict with other students, rather than having the teacher resolve the problems (the most common), and putting children in pairs or groups and having them work together to complete a project. Again, because the resolution of conflict is vital to good classroom management, the reason for implementing this goal may be tied more to immediate local necessity than to global values. Two similar items related to conflict and violence were seldom described or noted as being implemented in the classroom as frequently. These were identification of what contributes to conflict (Item 7) and study of people who have opposed conflict and violence (Item 13).

The items to which American teachers gave scant attention were the economic interconnectedness of peoples of the world (Item 2) and disparities among countries in production, distribution, and consumption of necessities (Item 14). Although Swedish teachers significantly more often identified these two goals as being implemented in their classrooms, they too seldom described how they implemented the goals. Considering the emphasis that American politicians, business leaders, and social studies educators place on these goals, it seems rather strange that so little attention is being given to them in our classrooms. Maybe Americans, because of their high economic status in the world, have not internalized economic interconnectedness and disparity. Perhaps teacher educators in both countries need to examine the emphasis being placed on these issues in their degree programs.

The difference between the two groups on the goal of religion (Item 20) is not surprising because there is no separation of church and state in Sweden as there is in the United States. Unfortunately America's effort to avoid espousing one religion over another appears to have left a void in the public school curriculum. Because most cultures and their related actions are closely intertwined with their religious heritage, it is questionable how much American students can truly understand diverse cultures not rooted in Christianity. This was probably most evident in the general public's lack of understanding of the complexities involved in the Persian Gulf conflict.

Teaching about the impact of technology on political, social, and economic conditions (Item 21) and teaching about forecasting change and designing alternative futures (Item 22) were seldom if ever described by either group. More often than any other areas, these two were seen as issues that should not be taught. Technology has been widely acclaimed as the vital link in preparedness for the future, yet its impact is seldom reflected on. My own observations of American classrooms suggest that technology is addressed more in terms of how to use it than in terms of how it will affect our lives in the long term. Technology's greatest impact will undoubtedly be felt as we struggle to make ethical and moral decisions regarding its use and distribution. If all this is true, educators need seriously to question their approach to technology in teacher education programs and the public schools.

The absence of the other issue from American and Swedish classrooms is of significant concern in my view because addressing this issue calls for higher-level thinking skills. Forecasting involves identification of trends, and analysis and evaluation of those trends. Developing alternative futures provides the opportunity for humankind to reflect on its past and have some sense of control over its future.

The teachers in this study were asked to describe how they were teaching about certain global issues. Their responses provide some insight into their understanding of what it means to teach with a global perspective. What some consider to be a global perspective may actually be more locally defined. For example, global items that directly affected the learning that took place in a classroom were described as being implemented more often than items that had farther-reaching and more long-term impact.

CONCLUSION

Global education has been in the literature for at least 20 years, yet American education is still not incorporating the goals of this movement into the curriculum. Although Swedish teachers may be implementing global issues in their curriculum more frequently than American teachers, the question remains, How are they doing this? A more in-depth look at Swedish classrooms and Swedish teacher education programs may provide some insight.

As educators struggle to identify their role in the new world order of the 21st century, they must carefully examine their goals and the methods used to accomplish the goals. If we truly seek to prepare our students to reflect on the changes that are taking place and to lead our world to higher levels of civilization, then we must specifically examine how well we are preparing teachers to address global issues. At the very least, this study challenges educators in both countries to examine their knowledge of global issues and their ability to incorporate these into the classroom. Although a well-developed curriculum is the most important tool for educational reform in any country and at any level, teachers' attitudes toward global education will ultimately determine its delivery and humankind's future.

REFERENCES

Altbach, P. G. (1989, Nov.). Needed: An international perspective. *Phi Delta Kappan,* 243–245.

Anderson, L. F. (1991). A rationale for global education. In *Global education: From thought to action* (1991 Yearbook of the Association for Supervision and Curriculum Development) (pp. 13–34). Alexandria, VA: Association for Supervision and Curriculum Development.

Bruce, G. M., Podenski, R. S., & Anderson, C. M. (1990). Developing a global perspective: Strategies for teacher education programs. *Journal of Teacher Education, 42*(1), 21–27.

Collins, H. T., & Zakariya, S. B. (1982). *Getting started in global education: A primer for principals and teachers.* Arlington, VA: National Association of Elementary School Principals.

Cornish, E. (1990). Issues of the '90s. *The Futurist, 24*(1), 23–26.

Hanvey, R. (1976). *An attainable global perspective.* Denver, CO: Center for Teaching International Relations.

Harris, A. C. (1986). *Child development.* New York: West Publishing Co.

Ramler, S. (1991). Global education for the 21st century. *Educational Leadership, 48*(7), 44–46.

Swedish National Board of Education. (1989). *Action programme for the internationalisation of education.* Stockholm: Swedish National Board of Education, Information Section.

Tucker, J. L., & Cistone, P. J. (1991). Global perspective for teachers: An urgent priority. *Journal of Teacher Education, 42*(1), 3–10.

Tye, K. A., & Kniep, W. M. (1991). Global education around the world. *Educational Leadership, 48*(7), 47–49.

Williams, W. W. (1988). *The effects of a global education inservice workshop on secondary social studies teachers' attitudes and perceptions of global issues.* Unpublished doctoral dissertation, University of Arkansas, Fayetteville.

APPENDIX 8-A
EXCERPTS FROM GLOBAL EDUCATION
QUESTIONNAIRE (SWEDEN)

Please respond to the following statements by circling the number that corresponds *best* with one of the following four statements.

4   Taught in my classroom

3   Should be taught in my classroom but is not now taught

2   Not taught in my class but in another one in my school

1   Should not be taught

1. Students are directly taught how to resolve conflict and controversy.   4 3 2 1

2. Students are taught that individuals, their towns, families, state and country have tangible economic connections with other nations and peoples of the world.   4 3 2 1

3. Students are taught that the earth's inhabitants have a common dependency on the way the planet works.   4 3 2 1

4. Students are taught that every human being on earth has the inherent right to a sense of self-worth.   4 3 2 1

5. Students are taught that citizen participation in government varies among political systems of the world.   4 3 2 1

6 Students are taught that literacy is the key to social mobility in their own country and a higher standard of living for all people.   4 3 2 1

7. Students are taught to be aware of those aspects of their culture which contribute to conflict and violence.   4 3 2 1

8. Students are taught that everyone on earth has the right to an equal share of the earth's resources.   4 3 2 1

9. Students are taught about the dangers to the ecology of the unlimited growth of population, land use, and energy consumption.   4 3 2 1

10. Students are taught to communicate with people from different backgrounds and heritages.   4 3 2 1

11. Students are taught the benefits as well as the difficulties inherent in a world of cultural diversity.   4 3 2 1

12. Students are taught that learning is a lifelong process.   4 3 2 1

13. Students study the lives of people who have opposed conflict and violence.   4 3 2 1

14. Students study the disparities of production, distribution, and consumption of necessities such as food among the countries of the world.   4   3   2   1

15. Students are taught to be responsible contributors to their present environment and the future global environment.   4   3   2   1

16. Students learn about human beings as a species—their common needs and expressions of emotion.   4   3   2   1

17. Students are taught to inquire into current world issues and analyze them objectively.   4   3   2   1

18. Students are taught that change is a constant in the world.   4   3   2   1

19. Students learn to recognize and accept that everyone's perception of the world is not necessarily the same.   4   3   2   1

20. Students study how religion impacts on the values and culture of different societies.   4   3   2   1

21. Students study the impact of technology on political, social and economic conditions of all the world's inhabitants.   4   3   2   1

22. Students are taught how to forecast change and design alternative futures.   4   3   2   1

Please describe briefly how you teach four of the items marked with a 4. List the number of the item and then describe how you cover this item in your classroom. For example: Item 9: "I use a simulation game in which the amount of space in the classroom available to the students keeps diminishing. We then discuss the results in relation to population control and wise use of land."

Item _____

_____

_____

Item _____

_____

_____

Item _____

_____

_____

Item _____

_____

_____

9
A LOOK ACROSS THE REPORTS TO A GLOBAL HORIZON: CONCLUDING COMMENTS
Brad West

"One world or none" may sound overstated and melodramatic to Americans, but to millions of other earth inhabitants, the concept cannot be overemphasized. Indeed, some say the powerful Golden Age of America has produced a citizenry that intellectualizes and rationalizes views of the rest of the world. We choose not to be very concerned with remote places that we have never been and remote peoples whom we have never met. This lack of concern is a common human characteristic and one that we hope this monograph will modify.

At the core the purpose of presenting these reports is to promote a heightened consciousness of the rest of the world, to call attention to the state of world conditions, to redirect energy toward an awareness of the diversity of cultures, and to provide a basis for understanding that global education is, quite simply, education for participation in an interdependent global society. The reports provide a basis for the following dictum:

> A global perspective requires the preparation of teacher educa-
> tors and teachers whose own knowledge about the world and

whose attitudes toward diversity and common human interests are consistent with global realities. (International Council on Education for Teaching, 1983)

In *Schooling for a Global Age*, Leestma (1979) writes that if teachers have the opportunity to become aware of the global facts of life and they then set about doing what they can within their spheres of influence, schools can make significant differences in how emerging generations meet the global issues of humanity, and they can contribute to shaping a future in which the human race will share a common destiny.

Future generations are counting on us to prepare educators with a global perspective; the ATE Task Force on Global Teacher Education believes that global perspectives should permeate all aspects of a teacher education program. However, getting from here to there is no simple task: Changed behavior (i.e., an enhanced global perspective) results from modified attitudes and beliefs. Generally, are Americans known for their ability to appreciate, to understand, and in some instances to tolerate or cope with other cultures? This monograph illustrates some ways in which some educators have altered their beliefs and discovered models of getting from here to there. Taking the chance that we will offend some, we will avoid the temptation so appealing to academics—the tendency to debate and become tangled in sticky webs of words such as *multicultural, diversity,* and *intercultural*—and get to the point:

- What does it mean to teach with a global awareness?
- What does such teaching require of teachers?
- What does such teaching require of teacher educators?

TEACHING WITH A GLOBAL AWARENESS

Teaching with a global awareness is easy in some classes (world history) and, some say, difficult in others. Is there no good answer to the question of how to teach globally in mathematics? In chemistry and physics? Foreign languages, of course, are naturals. What about physical education? Business? Are not music and art also perfect vehicles for global awareness? Vocational education? Social studies and English are replete with splendid possibilities. The illustration by Diane Sudbury can be conceptually duplicated in any elementary school grade or secondary school subject. The following examples from mathematics are offered:

The theory of graphs (plane figures in which lines join a set of points) is prominent these days: such networks attract

increasing attention, all the way from the iterative task of linking computers to the step-by-step analysis of the behavior of
interacting particles. The formal subject began with Leonard
Euler, by tradition with the seven bridges of staid Konigsberg
and the agreeable puzzle of how to enjoy a walk around town
that would cross each bridge only once.

The Eulerian path itself is the nub of children's games
among the Bushoog, a group who live around the capital of
the old Kuba chiefdom well east of modern Kinshasa in Zaire.

. . . .

And a final example:

The decimal base of many numeral systems surely begins with our 10 fingers and encourages mental excursions to
twenties and fives and their multiples and differences. But even
your own hands as a model are more complex than that. The
Yuki of California felt that their own number system arose
from the nature of the human hands although it is based on an
octal (8) base! Hold both hands before your eyes and count the
spaces between your fingers. The base 10 is no logical requirement of 10 fingers, although it is a probable choice. (Morrison,
1991, pp. 108–109)

Can any subject be taught with a global perspective? How many mathematics teachers introduce global concepts such as the preceding example into their
teaching? Whose responsibility is it to educate a math (or any other) teacher to
teach globally? If it is everyone's, is it also no one's?

THE VALUE OF THIS MONOGRAPH

This monograph is based on the idea that much can be learned by sharing
global experiences and insights. It supports the notion that teacher educators' interests in global perspectives can be aroused and that perhaps they can find incentives
to explore new ways to teach about living in a global community. For the internationally experienced, perhaps these pages will contribute to the development of new
adventures in global living. The reports amply demonstrate that participating in global opportunities is a first step in becoming global role models for students.

Four teacher educators have written about their expanded conceptual horizons. Trudi Osnes-Taylor's description of her personal effort to acquire a global

perspective is a splendid example of Leestma's (1979) point about doing what one can within one's sphere of influence; the process of going global is indeed the outcome. Elaine Jarchow and her family were ushered into the Maori culture in a *powfiri*, a formal welcoming ceremony in New Zealand, and left with vivid insights into personally held values of family, tradition, and the place of change. Two years of living in Egypt forever broadened Linda and Morgan Lambert's core understandings of what choice means. The experience also deepened their commitment to social activism.

Teacher educators sometimes experience a dilemma about global perspectives. On the one hand, there are demands from myriad special interests (special education groups, computer literacy organizations, etc.), strong influences from state departments of education, and pressure from a variety of external forces, all of which want certain learnings to be incorporated into an already tightly prescribed curriculum. On the other hand, there is a desire for international perspectives to be part of all teacher education programs. James Mahan and Laura Stachowski are national leaders in developing preservice intercultural and international field experience programs and in developing strategies to incorporate globalism into existing curricula. Students who student-teach in international programs, Mahan and Stachowski report, come into the profession armed with knowledge, insights, skills, strategies, and world perceptions that conventional programs are less likely to provide. Writing from the perspective of inservice teacher education, Patricia Betts Roach confronts a basic issue: Are Americans emotionally ready to deal with cultural differences? Embedded in her report is the observation that the teachers who participated in the international study trip to India that she codirected did not remember or did not believe to be true many of the cautions discussed before departure. Their preoccupation with truly immediate concerns resulted in unanticipated discomforts and disruptions. After the experience, however, insights were permanently fixed in their consciousness. They possessed new knowledge that would move them toward a more global point of view as they continued their teaching careers.

Diane Sudbury has woven a tapestry of global concepts into her seventh-grade world history classroom. Medieval European knights are contrasted with Japanese samurai; Michelangelo's painting is balanced with Yen Li-Pen's scroll art. Sudbury reinvents the Middle Ages for her students by emphasizing global concepts: The Middle Ages existed everywhere! This case study effectively shows a way to globalize a subject. Audrey Wright's research report suggests that Swedish teachers incorporate more global education issues and goals into their instruction than American teachers. The message is that unless we have teachers who are globally minded and globally aware, not much is going to happen. Americans are likely to come out on the short end of the global measuring stick for some time unless change in the classroom occurs soon.

DEVELOPMENT OF GLOBAL AWARENESS IN TEACHER EDUCATION PROGRAMS

Within their own spheres of influence, however, teacher educators can make a difference. We do not lack for opportunities to effect change:

• Global education courses for teachers can be found on practically every college and university campus. Inservice education days for teachers can be devoted to global education awareness, providing opportunities on site and within the working day. Curriculum specialists can help teachers examine their current curricula for global concepts and skills. Most communities have cultural festivals and events that invite everyone to participate. Certainly a major contributor to global awareness is professional travel, and vacation and holiday periods are replete with travel opportunities for teachers through low-cost charters, study tours, and seminars.

• In some ways development of global-mindedness in preservice teachers is less difficult than development of it in inservice teachers. Most undergraduate schools have choices within general liberal arts requirements that allow a student to focus on global education. Coordination among methods faculty relative to global aspects of their courses would surely aid in developing global sensitivities in future teachers. Undergraduates can participate in a wide range of experiences related to globalism: Often there is an office of international affairs on campus that helps coordinate activities of foreign students and promotes informal encounters between them and American students. Students can also be encouraged to participate in cultural fairs and festivals both on campus and in neighboring communities. Certainly student experiences abroad, even as tourists, will have an effect. Professional experiences in other countries, such as overseas student teaching, are generally available to every preservice teacher who wants them. Finally, there are experiences that have no equal, such as the work abroad programs and particularly the year abroad programs, many of which accept guest students from other universities and colleges.

• Teacher education faculty can take advantage of many similar opportunities and some unique possibilities. They are eligible for sabbatical leaves, exchanges, and visiting faculty positions, and they can apply for international fellowships and research grants. They can seek government, industry, or business sponsorship for international activities. Also, they are well positioned to ask questions about and develop proposals for globalizing teacher education in their institutions and beyond.

Faculty members can quickly determine the state of globalization on their campuses by reflecting on the *Guidelines for International Teacher Education* (AACTE, 1989). The guidelines consist of 103 questions grouped into seven areas: curriculum development, faculty development, student awareness, resources, administrative leadership, service, and research. For example, in curriculum development, one question is, "Are students in teacher education programs provided the opportunity to study, work or live in an international setting?" If the answer to this particular question is no, faculty can ask why this is the case and begin to change the answer to yes. The 103 questions are an institutional globalization thermometer.

This monograph, sponsored by the ATE Task Force on Global Teacher Education, is a collection of reports written by task force members and others. For teacher educators who are new to global education, the task force hopes that the reports arouse their interest and give them some incentive to seek out international opportunities. For individuals who are well traveled and knowledgeable about global living, the task force hopes that the reports introduce them to the notion that almost all subjects have a global perspective. In all cases the task force encourages teacher educators to pursue the ideas presented in these pages and to begin now or soon to infuse a global perspective into their professional practices.

The task force wishes to impart a dynamic interactive quality to this monograph by identifying resources and contacts for readers to use in advancing their own globalization. An appendix listing selected international education organizations and contacts follows. Readers are invited to connect with these organizations and individuals directly for further information on their respective international activities.

REFERENCES

American Association of Colleges for Teacher Education. (1989). *Guidelines for international teacher education.* Washington, DC: Author. (Address: One Dupont Circle, Suite 610, Washington, DC 20036-1186. $5.00 + $2.00 shipping and handling.)

International Council on Education for Teaching. (1983.) *A global perspective for teacher education* [Pamphlet]. Washington, DC: Author.

Leestma, R. (1979.) Looking ahead: An agenda for action. In J. M. Becker (Ed.), *Schooling for a global age.* New York: McGraw-Hill.

Morrison, P. (1991, Aug.). [Review of *Ethnomathematics: A multi-cultural view of mathematical ideas,* 1991, by M. Asher, Pacific Grove, CA: Brooks/Cole.] *Scientific American,* pp. 108–110.

APPENDIX 9-A
SELECTED INTERNATIONAL EDUCATION
ORGANIZATIONS AND CONTACTS
Brad West, compiler

Alliance for Education in Global and International Studies
45 John Street, Suite 1200, New York, NY 10038
Phone: 212/732-8606
　　　Links organizations, universities, projects, programs, school districts, and state departments of education working in precollegiate global and international education.

American Council on the Teaching of Foreign Languages
Six Executive Boulevard, Yonkers, New York
Phone: 914/963-8830

American Forum for Global Education
45 John Street, Suite 908, New York, NY 10038
Phone: 212/732-8606
　　　Publishes resource books (e.g., *International Studies Funding and Resources Book; Group Portrait: Internationalizing the Disciplines;* and *The New Global Yellow Pages,* a resource directory of 172 organizations that provide services related to international and global education), fundamental literature (such as *Internationalizing Your School*), curriculum materials, and materials from the National Clearinghouse on Development Education. Holds annual conferences and other meetings.

Association for Teacher Education in Europe
M. L. Kotterman, Administrative Officer, Rue de la Concorde 60, B-1050 Brussels,
　　Belgium
Phone: 32/2-514.33.40 • Fax: 32/2-514.11.72
　　　Publishes bimonthly newsletter with English translations; holds regional and annual meetings similar to those of ATE. Membership information available from ATE Council for International Affairs.

ATE Council for International Affairs
c/o Brad West, Chair, 116 Erickson Hall, College of Education, Michigan State
　　University, East Lansing, MI 48824
Phone: 517/353-0632 • Fax: 516/336-2795 • E-mail: BradWest@MSU.BITNET
　　　Administers general council business.

ATE Council for International Affairs, Committee for International Research

c/o Nancy Quisenberry, College of Education, Southern Illinois University, Carbondale,
   IL 62901

Phone: 618/453-2415 • Fax: 618/453-1646 • E-mail: GE1140@SIUCVMB.SIU.EDU

   Promotes networking among US and international teacher education researchers to
share findings, collaborate on studies, and inform members about government teacher education research projects. Facilitates ATE members' involvement in such projects and assists
ATE members in obtaining grant RFPs and resources for conducting international teacher
education research projects.

ATE Council for International Affairs, Committee for International Service

c/o Elaine Jarchow, College of Education, University of Nevada at Las Vegas, Las Vegas,
   NV 89154

Phone: 702/895-4851 • Fax: 702/895-4068 • E-mail: Jarchow@Nevada.Edu

   Serves as a clearinghouse of information on international teacher organizations and
funding/grant opportunities to develop international teacher education activities. Works co-
operatively with Committees on International Teaching and International Research to internationalize teacher education curricula, use locally available international resources, and
promote consulting opportunities for teacher education faculties.

ATE Council for International Affairs, Committee for International Teaching

c/o Sharon Brennan, College of Education, 1008 Taylor Building, University of
   Kentucky, Lexington, KY 40506-0001

Phone: 606/257-1857 • Fax: 606/258-1045 • E-mail: CPD434@UKCC.UKY.EDU

   Serves as a clearinghouse of information on international student teaching programs
and stateside "international" experiences for preservice teachers. Sponsors programs aimed at
sharing ideas about curriculum development and instructional practices with educators in
countries outside the United States through on-site visits and computer networks.

Center for International Education

US Department of Education, 7th and D Streets, S.W., Washington, DC 20202
Phone: 202/732-6061

   Administers several programs:

1. International Visitors Program.
2. International Studies Branch. Includes Fulbright-Hays programs, such as Group Projects
   Abroad, Seminars Abroad, and Bilateral Projects, and Title VI/Higher Education Act
   programs, such as the Undergraduate International Studies and Foreign Language Program and the Centers for International Business Education and Business and International Education.

3. Advanced Training and Research Branch. Includes Fulbright-Hays programs, such as Doctoral Dissertation Research Abroad and Faculty Research Abroad, and Title VI/ Higher Education Act programs, such as International Research and Studies, Language Resource Centers, National Resource Centers, and Foreign Language and Area Studies Fellowships.

Consortium for International Cooperation in Higher Education

One Dupont Circle, Suite 800, Washington, DC 20036

Phone: 202/857-1833

    Offers a central contact point for those outside the United States wanting access to American higher education.

Cooperative Projects in International Education

The Stanley Foundation, 420 East Third Street, Muscatine, IA 52761

Phone: 319/264-1500

Council on International Educational Exchange

205 East 42nd Street, New York, NY 10017

Phone: 212/661-1414

    Facilitates international education and youth study and travel through a variety of overseas travel, study, and work opportunities.

Council on International Exchange of Scholars

3007 Tilden Street, N.W., Suite 5M, Washington, DC 20008-3009

Phone: 202/686-6232

    Provides information on the Fulbright Scholar, Teacher Exchange, and Scholar-in-Residence programs.

The Experiment in International Living

Kipling Road, Brattleboro, VT 05301

Phone: 802/257-7751

    Promotes intercultural exchange programs; through the School for International Training, offers undergraduate and graduate programs in intercultural management, overseas refugee and community development and training programs.

Institute of International Education

809 United Nations Plaza, New York, NY 10017

Phone: 212/984-10017

    Sponsors educational and cultural exchanges.

International Council on Education for Teaching
2009 North 14th Street, #609
Arlington, VA 22201
Phone: 703/525-5253

Works to improve teacher education around the world; has held 40 world assemblies, the 41st being scheduled for July 1994 in Istanbul, Turkey.

National Association for Foreign Student Affairs
1860 19th Street, N.W., Washington, DC 20009
Phone: 202/462-4811

Promotes exchanges as educational resources to develop knowledge and appreciation. Publishes comprehensive newsletter and international publications.

People to People
501 East Armor Boulevard, Kansas City, MO 64109
Phone: 816/421-6343

Advances the cause of international friendship through voluntary efforts of private citizens.

ABOUT THE AUTHORS

JEAN L. EASTERLY is a professor of teacher education at California State University, Hayward, and the current chair of ATE's Task Force on Global Teacher Education. She has authored numerous chapters, monographs, articles, and simulation games, and has traveled widely. She recently served as the director of the East Bay International Studies Center.

ELAINE JARCHOW is an associate dean of the College of Education at the University of Nevada at Las Vegas. Formerly she was a faculty member at New Mexico State University. She chairs the Committee for International Service, a subcommittee of the ATE Council for International Affairs.

LINDA G. LAMBERT is the chair of the Department of Educational Leadership at California State University, Hayward. She and her husband Morgan Dale Lambert are writing about the changes in their perspectives that occurred as a result of their two-year experience in Egypt.

MORGAN DALE LAMBERT is an educational consultant currently working with schools in the San Francisco Bay area that are engaged in system reform. He is a former social studies teacher and also a former superintendent of schools in Marin County, California.

JAMES M. MAHAN is a professor in the Department of Curriculum and Instruction at Indiana University–Bloomington. He has conducted student teaching projects involving cultural immersion for over 20 years. Annually he works with about 100 students from Indiana University–Bloomington and 40 other participating colleges and universities.

TRUDI A. OSNES-TAYLOR is an associate professor in the Graduate Education Department at the University of St. Thomas in St. Paul, Minnesota. She is also a codirector of the Collaborative Urban Educator Program, a venture undertaken with the Minneapolis and St. Paul schools to prepare teachers of color for public school settings.

PATRICIA BETTS ROACH is a professor of secondary education at Arkansas Tech University. She teaches educational foundations at the undergraduate and graduate levels. A former Fulbright scholar who has traveled extensively in India, she is the president of the Arkansas Council for the Social Studies and the president-elect of the Arkansas Association of Teacher Educators.

LAURA L. STACHOWSKI is a visiting lecturer at Indiana University–Bloomington who is nearing completion of a PhD in curriculum and instruction. She is a former participant in Indiana University–Bloomington's Overseas Student Teaching Project and has been the project coordinator since 1981.

DIANE SUDBURY currently teaches eighth grade at Bret Harte Intermediate School in Hayward, California. She joined the faculty of the school in 1987 and has also taught seventh grade there. For the last three years Ms. Sudbury has been a mentor for the Hayward Unified School District.

BRAD WEST is a professor of teacher education at Michigan State University and a member of the staff of the Holmes Group. He chairs the ATE Council for International Affairs and is active in teacher education internationally, particularly through the Association for Teacher Education in Europe. He is the primary author of the international field experience guidelines in the American Association of Colleges for Teacher Education's *Guidelines for International Teacher Education.*

AUDREY E. WRIGHT is an associate professor of education in the Department of Curriculum and Instruction at Central Missouri State University. She currently teaches an experimental course at Vaxjo University in Sweden entitled Education in an Era of Global Change. She is also doing follow-up research on the study reported in this monograph, to determine the methods that Swedish teachers use to address global concepts.